Weaving a Canadian Allegory
Anonymous Writing, Personal Reading

Loretta Czernis

For centuries kings, political theorists, generals and cardinals thought of nations and institutions as social and corporate bodies. In this age of biotechnology, bodies are imagined as commodities that can be fixed. But the kind of mending required in the Canadian case is not like fixing a broken arm. It is much more tenuous and involves bringing citizens together not otherwise in touch with each other, who lack a sense of nationalism.

Loretta Czernis applies her sociological training in document analysis to study one government prescription for what ails Canadians. The *Report of the Task Force on Canadian Unity* rewrote Canada by reinventing patriotism, essentially inviting Canadians to imagine a new Canada. The *Report* itself is the product of what she calls the federal writing machine which exists to continually rewrite and thus reinvent Canada.

Czernis's contextural reading of the *Report* occurs on two levels. Reading technically, she examines the *Report*'s anonymous writing style that asks readers to imitate its own conclusions (be patriotic, buy a flag, shop at home).

Gestural reading invites reading as performance. Canadians are invited to participate in reshaping Canada by reading Canada allegorically, as a social body, capable of changing its form.

What a document may intend is not always the same as what is read into it. Mistakes can and do occur in the reading. Czernis suggests that these "mistakes" constitute a significant form of resistance to the anonymous writing machine.

Loretta Czernis teaches Sociology at Bishop's University in Lennoxville, Quebec.

Weaving a Canadian Allegory

Anonymous Writing, Personal Reading

by Loretta Czernis

Wilfrid Laurier University Press

Canadian Cataloguing in Publication Data

Czernis, Loretta, 1952-
   Weaving a Canadian allegory : anonymous writing,
personal reading

Includes bibliographical references and index.
ISBN 0-88920-232-X

1. Task Force on Canadian Unity.   2. Federal
government – Canada – Historiography.   3. Nationalism
– Canada – Historiography.   4. Governmental
investigations – Canada – Historiography.
I. Title.

FC98.C94 1994   971   C94-930418-2
F1027.C94 1994

WILFRID LAURIER UNIVERSITY PRESS
Waterloo, Ontario, Canada
N2L 3C5

Cover design by Jose Martucci, Design Communications

Cover illustration: *Smoke on the Water* by Marcel Saint-Pierre,
used with the permission of the artist.

Printed in Canada

Weaving a Canadian Allegory: Anonymous Writing, Personal Reading has
been produced from a manuscript supplied in electronic form by the
author.

Contents

Acknowledgements

This book has been published with the help of a grant from the Social Science Federation of Canada, using funds provided by the Social Sciences and Humanities Research Council of Canada.

Additional funding has been provided by Bishop's University.

I would also like to thank Dr. James Porter who supervised the doctoral dissertation from which this book emerged.

Preface

I taught the *Task Force Report* (also known as "Pépin-Robarts") when I was preparing a course on Canadian society as part of the summer curriculum at Algoma College in Sault Ste. Marie, Ontario. Presenting chapters from a research report on Canadian unity provided the students with some insight into one federalist version of Canada. More than this, reading the Report stimulated a great deal of heart-wrenching discussion about personal aspirations. Many of the students felt that there was a serious discrepancy between what they had been promised by the federal government and what they had actually received. One of these students was an Ojibwa woman. Two were steelworkers laid off by Algoma Steel after many years of committed service to the company. Two were homemakers. Along with three young full-time students, this group began a dialogue with me about Canada which was fuelled by our readings of the *Task Force Report*. I am deeply indebted to these students who inspired me to further this reading.

I tend to read a text as though I were studying the weave of a fabric. I came to recognize this pattern by studying the work of Mary Ann Caws, who has written much about the texture of texts. Written textures are subject to "the inconstant and obsessive co-constructions of observers and texts, where a roughness and deformation signal the high points of interest."[1] The written can also be read as a potential cloth, with some threadlike remnants ready to be woven, which will in turn inspire the spinning of new threads as writing.

A reader weaves colourful but unfashioned threads. All readings are situated in time, in space, and in particular con-

Notes to the Preface are on p. 113.

texts, inspired by particular persons, events, and/or prior readings. The facticity of a reading is the weaving process. Some of the findings that have emerged from reading as weaving indicate that in many textual studies, scholars have not acknowledged their positions as situated readers. To take responsibility for one's bodily context — to remember that as analyst one is still only and always a particular reader, with one pair of eyes and one imagination — to know one's limits is to have a thesis. The thetic is the place where one begins because a reader can only ever start where (s)he is — situated in a particular context.

It is possible to produce multiple readings of a text. A reader can assume more than one distinct reading position in relation to a given text. Once freed from the constraints of the categories of "correct" reading, the reader can move from a rigid and technical frame into a contextural one. Multiple reading reveals multi-level writing strategies. Those employed in the Task Force policy documents are facets of a style that is characterized by a call to the "we," to participate in the taking of an oath and to reorient to kinship. As will be discussed, many rhetorical strategies have been employed within the *Task Force Report* which appropriate terms, concepts, and images in the interest of rewriting Canada as an appealing social icon. The context is undermined by this *Report*'s obsessive focus on the production of a particular version of unity. Nevertheless, the context can be retrieved by the reader who negotiates a gestural reading.

An anonymous writing style maintains aspects of a feudal consciousness. Canada, as rewritten in the *Task Force Report*, is an example of a social emblem, an iconographic construction that emerges from within an abstract symbolic discourse that seeks a narrative history. To this end, Canada's traditions are rewritten by the federal writing machine in an allegorical mode. However, it will be demonstrated below that allegory is a genre that suspends precedent. The federal discourse on unity produces writings that search for a past in a simulation of what is imagined to have been before, but which was never there. It is only here, in the Task Force's new writing about Canada. The country must now be "re"membered as the strong body of old Canada, before it was diagnosed as an ill body/bodies and given a prognosis in which the *Task Force Report*'s prescription for unity is considered essential. The descriptions of social bodies, the diagnosis, and the prescription are entirely the creations of the *Task Force Report*.

The Task Force documents can be read so as to view their allegorical texture, which is ahistorical. Yet allegory has been used as a writing strategy in the interest of rewriting Canada's history. Allegory is a potent form which overflows beyond the intended readings of Task Force writers. The excess generates more and diverse possible readings. This policy-writing about Canadian unity yearns for traditions that must be continually rewritten.

The vision presented in the *Task Force Report* of the various versions of Canada — those defined as unified and not, as sick or well, and the old and then the new — emerge from a discourse presented as both caring and anonymous. The word anonymity describes the position of researchers who do not hear, who limit their perceptual capacities by writing for/to citizens in a federally approved policy style. Those readers who adopt this style in their own writings or who believe that this style represents their concerns are also rendered anonymous. One significant effect of anonymity in policy is a deafness to alternative discursive forms, such as the local, native, and minority interests, which are downplayed, while special attention is paid to a loud proclamation for the generic "we." The speech of local persons who retain associative versions of Canada is viewed as being hostile to unity, and to non-citizens, because writing directed at (and by) no one creates a moral vacuum outside of which there are no citizens. Subjects can only be recognized as participants inside of the federal discourse on unity.

The *Task Force Report* was written by a number of civil servants (some full-time and others contracted); therefore, it is not productive to find one writer and ask her/him what was intended. Even if I were to contact the over 100 persons who researched and wrote this document, it would be impossible to retrace their collaboration. However, it is possible to assume that something was intended by this writing, and intentions regarding issues of writing and reading are ques-

tions of style. The Task Force writers have transcribed a discourse that was developed before their writing, and which
may continue long after they retire. It is also a way of writing that invites anonymity from readers, but this need not,
and does not, always happen. Anonymous reading, by its
nature, implies the relinquishing of one's ability to discrimi-
nate; it may be, however, that one cannot give up one's
uniquely developed reading skills, which involve, among
other things, comparing and choosing. As Bruce Curtis has
shown, even social actors who are functionally illiterate can
be critical readers of government policy.

The power of a story was once attributed to its teller; in
many stories, as in the *Task Force Report*, no distinct teller
remains. So, left with the page (or the screen), listeners have
become readers anxious to take up the text as if it were a living, breathing presence lonely for conversation. There is
much debate over whether there is life in the written, and
what the nature of this vitality might be. Assuming the loss
of the writer's identity as a result of oppressive and bankrupt
discourses, I am reading for what remains. I have found
these remains to be remnants, tattered or unravelled threads
of narrative genres and oral traditions. This kind of seeking
as reading is not anonymous. It is a dialogue which twines a
unique consciousness and fringes of cultural competence,
both drawing from and adding to ignorance/knowledge.
What emerges from this dialogue is experienced by the reader as her/his context. This is the perceptual, situated experience of reading textures. The search for and weaving of
threads is necessary while reading in order to get at contex-
ture. To seek such threads, I will argue, is a way of finding
one's context, in the course of which a document can come to
life as a conversation with both collectively memorized
archetypes and newly imagined characters. The reflexive
attempt to describe and frame this interactive procedure,
and thereby some aspects of the models which inform it, can
be understood as reading contexturally.

Making present what is other (and sometimes ancient) in
dialogue creates it anew, and serves as a comparison to
taken-for-granted reading practices. Comparison (when something that is "commonly known" is restated as a problem —

when it becomes a question) is a critical activity. Alternative questions make for the possibility of discrimination, disagreement, argument, and eventually, perhaps, new knowledge/ignorance. Sociological practice is fuelled by desire — the desire to better oneself by helping to improve conditions for others. Doing something for the better means that one must first compare and contrast what one sees and hears. Weaving requires that threads be in a state of tension, which occurs when they originate from contrasting angles. The primary concern of the contextural analyst therefore,

> is to point to the surface, with its implied tension, and to some connecting threads. This double exposure to the visual and the verbal, by repeated acquaintance or in the rapid flicker of a nervous gaze, is meant to illuminate the play and attractions of text and mind, which a passionate reading informs.[2]

Introduction

News about Canada, the Uncountry

This book is about reading a set of government documents created by the Task Force on Canadian Unity in 1979. The eight persons whose signatures appear at the beginning of each of the three volumes are Jean-Luc Pépin, who, along with John P. Robarts, co-chaired the Task Force, Gerard A. Beaudoin, Richard Cashin, Solange Chaput-Rolland, Muriel Kovitz, Ross Marks, and Ronald L. Watts. The work of this Task Force was widely publicized in newspapers and magazines in 1978 and 1979, and then it was forgotten. Looking back at these documents one glimpses how everything changes and yet everything stays the same.

Peter C. Newman wrote in *Maclean's* in 1979 that there was some good news from the Task Force on Canadian Unity: "Canada, the uncountry, can be reinvented."[3] Who, or what has been attempting this reinventing? I argue that there exists a federal writing machine. Not a machine made of steel, but a machine made of people who continuously modify the machine in order to keep it functional. I suggest that Canada is continually being reinvented by being rewritten, which has happened more than once. The 1979 *Task Force Report* is interesting to consider because it rewrites Canada by reinventing patriotism. In this book I argue that the *Task Force Report*: (1) invited readers to think of the past and present Canada as three bodies, and (2) gave citizens written intructions as to how they should imagine a new Canada as an entirely different entity than the existing duality generated by the French and English founding peoples.

Notes to the Introduction are on p. 113.

These strategies for imagining Canada require two of the types of rewriting outlined by Jean-François Lyotard. First, rewriting can be a re-examination and further analysis of historical events to discover new elements in them. "It is frequently the case that 'rewriting modernity' is understood in this sense, the sense of remembering, as though the point were to identify crimes, sins, calamities engendered by the modern set-up — and in the end to reveal the destiny that an oracle at the beginning of modernity would have prepared and fulfilled in our history."[4] Here we can substitute the word modernity for the word Confederation. Second, "Rewriting can consist . . . of starting the clock again from zero, wiping the slate clean, the gesture which inaugurates in one go the beginning of the new age and the new periodization."[5]

The image of the body has long been associated with the state. For centuries, kings, political theorists, generals, and cardinals thought of nations and institutions as social and corporate bodies. In this age of biotechnology, bodies are imagined as commodities that can be fixed. But the kind of mending required in the Canadian case is not like setting a broken arm. The problem is much more ephemeral. It involves bringing citizens together who are not only physically separated from one another, but who also lack a sense of nationalism. *The Report of the Task Force on Canadian Unity* attempted to write a prescription for what ailed citizens then, and still ails them now. Studying its three volumes has given me an opportunity to develop a unique perspective on recent Canadian history on the issues of unity and nationhood. This perspective, combined with my sociological training in document analysis, has taught me that task forces and commissions do not have the cure for what ails us, although it is an essential part of their mandates to diagnose. Task force reports, politicians, and the formulas thought up by lawyers and political scientists, come and go, but there can be no new solutions while everything is processed through the same writing machine.

What do I mean about this writing machine being "the same"? Compare the work of Joe Clark's Special Joint Committee on a Renewed Canada to the work of Pierre Trudeau's Task Force on Canadian Unity. Their mandates are very similar. The Task Force was supposed to "go to the public and seek its views."[6] The Joint Committee was supposed "to seek your views on the government's proposals, entitled 'Shaping Canada's Future.'"[7] Although Clark's committee was more overtly engaged in constitutional debate, both committees employed the same language: Canada has a shape, but, in order to have a future, Canada must be reshaped. Canadians are then asked to imagine various shapes for Canada. This is the ongoing work of the writing machine.

Certain shapes are emblematic. The remembrance of the nation's body is often invoked by a flag. Canada's 100th birthday gave the government a chance to show off the country's new flag. On Canada's 125th birthday, you could buy a different kind of Canadian flag. This flag celebrated and commemorated *Canada 125*, and cost between $20 and $35. Souvenirs were pushed very heavily on Canada's recent birthday. The idea is similar to buying a relic to come into immediate contact with a saint. If you buy a flag you own a piece of Canada. To own a flag is to participate. To participate is to be patriotic. Even if you do not feel patriotic, you can buy participation. This, too, is the ongoing work of the writing machine. The advertising for the *Canada 125* celebration was somewhat slicker than it had been in 1967, for Canada's 100th birthday. Civil servants are well trained in marketing. They know how to promote flags, coffee cups, Canada Day events, and committee hearings. These are all patriotic experiences. Wear a T-shirt, or watch Special Joint Committee hearings on television. Involvement is made easy; it has become painless to be proud of Canada. Just buy a *Canada 125* tote bag and then it becomes obvious who is patriotic. This has also become true of the ways in which CBC newscasters constantly remind us of the sin of cross-border shopping. As our social body is constantly weakened by the large parasite to the south, we are instructed to defend ourselves by shopping at home. The parasite at home, called the GST, is less evil than the one called the United States because our taxes keep our country going, or so they tell us.

This sermon is heard but Canadians, being extremely clean and cautious people, do not like parasites in any form. As will be explained, in federal documents such as the *Task*

Force Report, citizens were told that péquistes and radical regionalists were parasites making Canada weak and ill. Paying the GST weakens the bank accounts of ordinary Canadians, who are justifiably afraid during these dark economic days. Why not keep one's pocketbook closed to those who ask a higher price for the same item? Why is it suddenly better to throw money away? The government says that this money helps the country, but most citizens see no evidence of such help. So they look to the cheaper parasite, which seems to drain them less.

What a document may intend is not always the same as what is read into it. The writing machine asks that citizens act for Canada; if they cannot motivate themselves to care, they can at least buy a flag or pay a GST. But one does not always agree to do what one has been asked. And if the message is ambiguous, all kinds of misunderstandings can result, some of which may be suprisingly innovative. I also discuss such "mistakes" in this book, and suggest that they constitute a significant form of resistance to the anonymous machine.

1 *Concerning Contexture*

Reading can be a method of weaving wherein the threads come not just from words on a page, but from context as well. Context is composed of remnants of other, prior readings that are entwined anew by particular readers. Reading as weaving discloses and creates something both old and new. To read self-consciously in this manner is what I call the production of a contextural analysis, which involves "The act of weaving or assembling parts . . . [and/or] an arrangement of interconnected parts; a structure."[8] One can generate a structure that is both old and new by producing a double reading of a text, one that is both technical and gestural.

Communication is fundamentally relational, and very often reading can evoke non-verbal imagery of a non-rational form. Imagery that is created in the mind's eye has a more immediate, intuitive impact, because it operates on a textual/textural surface that can be called gestural.

It is possible, when one has seen a gestural surface in a writing, that is, the production of images that spring from the written and the reader, to relate a text to kinship, which involves linking documentary emblems to fragments of collective memory. In the case of the *Task Force Report*, the emblems resonate in allegory. The allegory traces a ragged path through the canon of policy knowledge to the memory of calamity, here identified as the end of Canada.

"It is an old cliché to say that Canada was knit together in defiance of geography."[9] There are two emblematic references in this passage. The first relates to knitting, which is

---

Notes to Chapter 1 are on p. 113.

also to be associated with stitching, and suturing. The second reference is to geography. Here the land, as well as sectors of Canadian society, are imagined to have been joined together with procedures involving the use of thread—the thread of citizenship, and of a sympathetic reading of federal versions of Canadian history. The image of Canada being held together through constant processes of ideological stitching is dashed in a later chapter, when it is stated that "the spectacle of Canadian governments wrangling constantly among themselves has done nothing to reduce cynicism about public affairs and it has presented Canadians with the image of a country deeply divided against itself."[10] The stitches in Canada's skin are thus torn apart by ongoing debate, here referred to as incessant "wrangling." The emblem is Canada's geography as a body with skin. The skin contains sutures which are easily separated by "wrong" argument.

Contextural analysis of a text makes reading a participation in rhetorical persuasion. Reading then becomes a performance in which one hopes to regenerate the kinship text by misreading (in order to revive a socially meaningful identity) as a heuristic procedure (to be explained in detail in chapter 2). Essential to contextural analysis is the ability to watch oneself read, for to observe one's reading performance can reveal complex perceptual and imaginative gestures worthy of consideration. A bifocal approach (cultural and individual; political and literary) is also necessary in order to break through the confines of reading as a purely technical, information-absorbing activity. The distinction between the approaches is made explicit by the contextural reading of the *Report* in chapters 3-6, set against the Appendix.

My reading of the *Task Force Report* moves between the policy research surface of the work, and an allegorical surface. The *Report* was written in order to generate interest in, and pave the way for, the repatriation of the Constitution. Yet in order to amend/create a new Constitution, the history of Canada had to be rewritten in such a way as to appeal to a significant portion of the Canadian population in an immediate and memorable fashion; the symbolism that was chosen is derived from medieval allegorical narrative strategies, most noticeably in the usage of the concept of duality.[11] Gestural reading for contextural analysis brings these medieval aspects of kinship connection in the text to the foreground. As will be shown, Quebec is set against Canada as its double. The double is developed as a lesser aspect. The technical surface of the *Report* is linear, and seems to present only one viewpoint, from one anonymous writer. The policy only gains texture if one reads for the contrasting threads. One way to look for rhetorical strategies and devices in the documents is to begin by thinking of the sentence subjects as operating on one level and the predicates advancing from another.

> It may be observed that of the disjunction customarily attributed to allegory that the literal level is conveyed by the predicates, the allegorical or metaphoric level by the personified nouns. Thus when it is claimed that allegory says one thing and means another, it is the predicates that "say" the one [relates] and the (personified) nouns that "mean" the other [duality].[12]

In this particular text, the nouns have "voices," and the verbs see, but cannot hear. The nouns are capable of speech, but their voices are made active by the policy initiatives of their predicates. The nouns are therefore passive protagonist/foils who speak and listen as descriptive ciphers for a rewritten Canada. As will be shown in chapter 4, metaphors in allegory form a parabolic backdrop or ground before which policy terminology can serve as a figural element. Anthropomorphized moral symbols, such as the three Canadas, depicted as three protagonist/foils, create the allegorical surface of the *Task Force Report*. The technical surface of policy is shown in the predicates, which fulfill their direction by animating their subjects. The three social bodies developed in this policy-writing serve as stark sentries of good and evil through "whom" Canadian unity "evolves."

As will be demonstrated in the reading analysis, *The Report of the Task Force on Canadian Unity* is a reporting of state fragmentation that prescribes a model for national integration. Task Force writers have compensated for that fragmentation by constructing Unity as an allegorical symbol. A new Canada is not only prescribed, it is proscribed, as the only iconic solution. New Canada is thus accompanied by new thinking on unity. This thinking is a ritual of allegiance and a formula for attempting to convey to reader-citizens how they may best serve their country—by thinking of themselves, and their facticity, as being vitally linked to a country such that it becomes more intensely recognized by them as being their own. This is the subjection of living communities to written rules, which is emphasized by evoking a fear of calamity—the death of Canada. The prevention of calamity is treated as an issue of survival (members will not survive unless the state's body is sustained), and as a focal point for the gathering of allegiance: think of only one Canada, one image of a unified nation. Other, more regional, ethnic, or native-based images provoke conflict, and must therefore be avoided. According to the Task Force, conflict arises from dwelling on the analysis of particular concerns; the analysis of difference (as a wrong reading) splits thought, and this, the reader is warned, can put an end to Canada. The *Report of the Task Force on Canadian Unity* maintains that Canada can only survive if it is thought of as unified, if the reader attends to the thought of the state as one unit, and produces a unified, anonymous reading of Canada.

For readers to believe that doom is near, they must be capable of believing that the social bodies that have been written about are "real." Allegorical style provides a version of history for this purpose. It is a strategy for writing that relies heavily on the imagination, looking for cognitive legitimation by way of the mental lexicon's list of symbolic protagonists and their adventures. It is a style which cannot accommodate polyphony, its harmony being based upon a linear narrative morality that does not accommodate multiple realities. For this reason, allegory is an appropriate style for a writing committed to unity as a primary discursive effect. More than one social body causes conflict; therefore, a battle must be fought and resolved in order to regain the stability of attending to one state icon.

> The fundamental narrative forms of allegory are the journey, battle or conflict, the quest or search, and transformation: i.e., some form of controlled or directed process. The control is provided by the object of the journey, combat or quest: we interpret the significance of the "motion" of the

characters and the forces affecting them in the light of knowledge about the direction in which they travel.[13]

The *Task Force Report*'s allegorical model that forms old and new histories, and thereby various versions of Canadas, appears to "move forward" into a more unified Canada. The semblance of movement is produced by writing about the fragmentation of symbolic confederate and conflict versions of Canada's body. These other ways of conceptualizing Canada are ultimately discounted as practically impossible alternatives to the new Canada, which is described as a body of Unity. In writing that certain iconic bodies (namely, the confederate and conflict versions of Canada) are degenerating and in need of restructuring, the *Report*'s narrative relies upon disintegration in order to relay a sense of urgency. This way of writing movement (Unity as the phoenix rising out of the ashes of the old Canada) produces further complexity: ethnic and native interests only become recognizable in relation to Unity. Yet Unity, as the allegorical protagonist, can only emerge out of the figures which are described in the document as producing discord. Throughout the *Task Force Report*, multiple interpretations of the shape of Canada are made to conflict, are diagnosed, condescended to, levelled, and suppressed. The anonymous style can only accommodate harmony as oneness — one state with its accompanying coda — the discourse on Unity.

The *Task Force Report*'s ideal future Canada and its vision of patriotism, important to the growth of the body of Unity, can be seen as a series of written images that struggle to address the projections of reader-citizens. Yet allegory is an ambiguous style. The attempts to match obscure personifications with enigmatic events lend themselves to the possibility of misreading. Misreading can carry the reader from technique to a gestural perspective: to perform a misreading is to create meaning; creative interpretation involves self-conscious performance of cultural competencies and conventions. This form of attention can also be called ritual. It is possible to ritually engage the context of writing by exploring the multivalent aspects of reading. To do so involves developing a gestural relation to texts. A well-developed gestural relation will help the reader to activate and analyze textu(r)al aspects of kinship. But how does this become contextural analysis? Building such a reading performance into an analysis with a structure is not easy. The urge to structure is a desire to communicate what has been discovered in reading. But what kind of structure is adequate? How do I complete a recognizable piece of cloth in the form of a contextural analysis? There are many tools available in many different disciplines, and each promises to be the completely adequate instrument for textual research.

No one theorist has adequately explained my experience of reading the *Task Force Report*. Thus it became necessary for me to appropriate aspects of different kinds of studies so that I could articulate what and how I was reading. My approach is a particular attitude of reading for style, since style communicates, by its very structure, a relationship to that which has been written. It becomes possible to conceive of relations to the written when it is remembered that "relation" is a term that not only refers to kin, but also to the act of telling, and to accounts of many types. Relations are fundamentally discursive; an act of telling, of relating, is an attempt to seek/assert kinship, for kinship is universal and is based not only upon blood ties but also upon marriage and other forms of alliance. Even citizens are called upon by their nation as children are called upon by parents/elders to help in times of crisis. This is a way of asking people to extend their interest beyond the sphere of their immediate families and to care for their country as if for a relative in need.

2 *Reading and Projection*

Sociologists have recently become interested in texts as sites for the investigation of many types of interaction. Discoveries made about reading and writing have indicated the ways in which social researchers have read texts, and how they then assume others read. Technical and gestural reading can be thought of as two different attitudes towards interaction. Technical reading is a formal, businesslike, win-or-lose approach. Gestural reading is open-ended, playful, and desires that both reader and text "win" in that they are both made richer creatively. To see writing only as means to an end, a commodity to be pressed for information and then discarded, is to participate in a perspective that would also, for example, see friends as disposable. Discounting writing as merely manipulatable and disposable also implies a similar judgment for the reader, and for one's own reading.

Bryan Green's book, *Knowing the Poor*, is an analysis of the (British) *Poor Law Report of 1834* and the *Majority and Minority Poor Law Reports* of 1909. Green argues that within these documents "poorness" shifted from being the subject of a description to the object of an oppressive set of administrative practices. In the 1834 *Report*, to be poor had meant to be lacking or deprived in some way which was temporary. By 1909, being poor became an identifier, a legal category which became, for the people so designated, a permanent label, a kind of discursive tattoo. The poor were transformed by an appropriation of "poorness" in policy.

Notes to Chapter 2 are on pp. 113-14.

They became an anonymous mass who had to fit into the category before the eyes of the law.

> At the heart of every production process is an empty core around which the product forms. . . . "The reader" is imaginable as such an empty core or place at the heart of writing as a productive process. The methods of a text (its generic conventions, stylistic devices and so on) can then be thought of as ways of drawing the reader who reads into that place.[14]

The reader can be understood to be a commodity, a "virtual reader" when (s)he is assumed to have no ability whatsoever to choose an alternate way of reading. There are as many ways to be poor as there are ways to read and interpret laws. Green is predominantly concerned with what he takes texts to intend, assuming that texts unfold as clear and concise sets of instructions for readers to take up so as to assist the text's desired construction of reality. Green's "empty core" is a space awaiting a reader, one who will answer the call to what is intended by proceeding as the text supposedly instructs. Yet as Green also points out, no text offers a complete set of instructions. Readers are always left with some interpretive problems.

Green's writing dignifies, privileges, the problem of a space, an emptiness, a lack. Green does not adequately explicate his own reading process, so that I am left in a quandary as to the full extent of his meaning of emptiness. How is it that he needed to find gaps to fill in? As a text analyst, did he create the gaps which he thought that he would need to find, both for himself and for other readers? Does he interact with texts through empty space — through what is not there? If so, it is a startling and very interesting interactive reading problem to which an essay could be solely devoted.

Ken Morrison's "'Telling-Order Designs' in Didactic Inquiry" is a study that explores how textbook articles lead readers to specific facts by way of anticipated readings which are assumed to preoccupy the writers. The reader is posited as having extremely limited interpretive options,[15] being continually confronted by "knowledge" objects such as technical terms in textbooks. Morrison does not write of options to be considered by readers. He refers instead to the designs that present facts to be found in the written material. Reading for him seems a bit like hunting for buried treasure, looking for the key words that demarcate what he takes to be the "sequential resources of a writing system."[16] The type of sequence he assumes is gravitational. That is, he assumes writings are read downwards, linearly following sentences and paragraphs.

Morrison's conception of a written page is very helpful; however, his formulation of sequence may be misleading. The findings of cognitive theorists and ethnomethodologists confirm that, depending upon specific text and context, many people do not read sequentially (see next section). Instead, our eyes want to dart all over the place much of the time during reading. Therefore one need not be ashamed if one does not read the newspaper page by page. Evidently, the curiosity that makes a reader flip to the back or the middle of a work is an important part of reading.

Two people may not take the same writing "seriously"; hence, some readers will be comfortable flipping through a work while others will read in depth. Furthermore, it is possible that different kinds of texts will be read differently: the same text can be read both formally and informally, as information or fiction, depending on the reader. In his article, Morrison writes about a certain kind of linear and gravitational writing sequence in a selection of academic texts through which readers are supposedly "led." Green writes about what is virtual, as well as about the gaps anticipated by writing, which he assumes to have "the constitutive power . . . to formulate the reader it requires."[17] Is there a tendency, or a pressure, to read academic/legal documents in a more linear fashion than more "informal" works? These questions cannot be adequately answered until more reading studies are produced.

In his article "The Speller Expelled: Disciplining the Common Reader in Canada West," Bruce Curtis hypothesizes that adults and children in Canada West during the 1850s were unhappy about becoming literate. This "artisanal reaction" to formal education on the part of agrarian communities is assumed by Curtis to be a form of intuitive resistance to the politics of reading.

> Literacy, I will be concerned to argue, was as much a polit-
> ical-economic phenomenon as the buying and selling of
> labour power. . . . Individual psychology was seen, in the
> most general terms, as a moral economy whose motive
> forces could be structured in keeping with political-eco-
> nomic objectives. . . . The politics of literacy aimed to trans-
> form the reality of social experience through transforma-
> tions of individual character structure.[18]

Those who, more than a century ago, had little motiva-
tion to read, may have mistrusted books, understanding
them to be foreign objects that were given great importance
by strangers. When the strangers tried to enforce reading,
the illiterate community also exerted force. Theirs was the
power to mistrust, to understand the code without reading
its signifiers — to see the code itself as a signifier, a herald of
community fragmentation. And what does it mean today that
so few citizens are interested in reading policy documents?

In "The Active Text" Dorothy Smith describes how social
acceptance of different written versions of an event is such
that one version comes to represent a "mandated course of
action." This account constitutes the "real," or the "factual,"
account because its writers make the document seem official
to readers. The official version "marks a shift from one order
of relations to another, from the actual organizational practices to the public textual discourse in which they become
known and interpreted to 'citizens.'"[19] Smith's interest is not
in texts per se, but in how textual practices can change the
ways in which actual persons relate to one another in everyday life. She contends that documents have become a form of
currency which dominates the sense-making practices of
"sophisticated" social actors in their public textual relations.
Dorothy Smith does not address reading directly. How a particular reader employs documentary currency is of interest to
her only in relation to circulation, that is, whether or not
readers and writers interactively engage in ongoing reality
construction (and the problems that may arise when they do
not). Documents constantly mediate the negotiated articulation of reality.

I read Smith as follows: Those who want to be successful
try to figure out how the system works. They learn to take

up the "right" writing, and reading, in order to align themselves with what they take to be important and powerful. In
the process they also undergo a shift: instead of acting as
particular readers, they choose to become anonymous ones.
This is not to say that it is always easy to remain true to
one's particularity. Readers and writers who do not participate appropriately in documentary exchange can be margin-
alized and categorized by officials who presume to have cor-
nered the market on what is real. Unique readers can be
labelled as illiterate, or even crazy. Stigmatized readers can
weaken due to abuse. When written currency is given a privileged position over and against lived experience, reading
subjects become read objects. The subject participates in
turning her/himself into a commodity, an instrument of documentary reality. Every member is read and written.

Beng-Huat Chua extended the sociological analysis of
texts into the domain of Canadian public policy study with
his work on the *Royal Commission on Bilingualism and
Biculturalism* (hereafter, the *B & B Commission*). Chua discovered through his analysis that this *Report* was designed
to convince citizens of certain facts, and was therefore written in an evidentiary style. Evidence has thus become
currency in documents for Chua. Evidence indicates what is
best for the majority. The majority is what concerns the
federal government. Local and particular interests have no
use-value if they cannot engage in the appropriate national
forms of exchange:

> An ongoing concern of the liberal democratic state is to con-
> vince its members that it is operating in the best interest of
> every member whenever possible, even if this "best inter-
> est" may often result in personal hardships for some seg-
> ment of the society.[20]

Actual writers in Chua's analysis are spoken of as "it"
(the anonymous writers who work for the "liberal democratic
state"), and actual readers are viewed as virtual citizens
("every member"). Chua assumes that the text contains a
single set of fixed meanings as signified. He does not enter-
tain the idea that he, as a highly trained text analyst, could
bring an idiosyncratic reading into his analysis, unless he
prefers to think of himself as another anonymous "it" (which

is how I read him). The *B & B Commission* in Chua's analysis becomes an example, a subset of bureaucratic inscription, an isolated and isolating fixture carved in stone as it were. The text cannot be negotiated. There are not even any gaps. It is a monolith, with recursions, that is, identical replicas of itself at different levels. Writers work with chisels. Readers beg for a little information and are given permission to briefly touch the model. This linear and decontextualized form of analysis reifies the reading subject.

In John O'Neill's *Essaying Montaigne*, the reader is described as an "institution" that participates in multiple realities, juggling anonymity and meaning-making simultaneously.

> We encroach upon one another, borrowing from each other's time, words and looks that we are looking for in ourselves. In this way, our mind and self may be thought of as an institution which we inhabit with others in a system of presences which includes Socrates or Montaigne as much as our own present friends.[21]

O'Neill's description of subjectivity as sharing is a reminder of the delicate intricacies involved in human interaction. In much of this book O'Neill is concerned with the construction of a documentary archaeology concerning how Montaigne read, and how he has been read; yet O'Neill does not address the activity of reading directly. In the chapter on "Rival Readings" he asks,

> How can the "Essays" have provoked such starkly opposed conclusions? Is there no middle ground? We, of course, could not mean by this that there is some way of withholding interpretation. Rather, what we have in mind is the question how is it we are able to move among rival readings, attacking here and holding our ground there.[22]

Does this imply that O'Neill disagrees with many other text analysts? He has asserted that one text can produce opposing viewpoints. However, the positions of which he writes do not include the gestural reading attitude of the present study. Reading, for O'Neill, seems to be a warfare in which he finds himself surrounded by "rival" readings, from which he must distinguish those that are friendly from those that are adversarial. He seems to be fighting with the text and former interpreters, hoping to "win" his own interpretation by killing off others, whom he previously admitted to needing in order to develop and maintain subjectivity. But if subjectivity is sharing, to kill off the rest is to kill oneself. O'Neill thus seems to me to be a self-destructive reader. I am still trying to surmise what he (bracketing his insistent "we"), and many of the text analysts I have previously mentioned, actually do when they read. I can only surmise, since these writers do not make their reading practices explicit for consideration. Reading can be studied as speech, movement, and emotions have been. Self-presentation continues without others; one can present oneself before a text in a number of ways. The reader can be a sender, a receiver, or both. To be both is to hear and to speak, to weave one's experience with work written by those who wish to remain, in the case of policy-writing, nameless. The reader who does not take the opportunity to be equal to the text's authority will remain voiceless:

> Tone and force signify the present voice: they are anterior to the concept, they are singular, they are, moreover, attached to vowels . . . when the subject is there in person to utter his [*sic*] passion. When the subject is no longer there, force, intonation, and accent are lost in the concept.[23]

Alex McHoul has made some interesting discoveries in his attempts to study his reading practices. In his book *Telling how texts talk*, he applies various tests to texts, including a detailed ethnography of the act of reading a newspaper article, which was recorded on tape. The tape was then transcribed and analyzed for significant features. He discovered that prior experience with reading the newspaper does not necessarily mean that a reader will automatically know how to read every article. Readers are literate, but are continually called upon to (re)organize and (re)learn how they know.

> Rules are not objects of knowledge — they are not known but followed. . . . [W]e should say both (1) that a particular occurrence of a rule's being followed will by no means admit us immediately to all such occasions and concomitantly (2) that following the rule will not mean that we are

pre-prepared for some particular occasion of its jurisdiction prior to (or "outside") that occasion being interactively constructed.[24]

McHoul posits that newspaper readers both know and don't know how to read articles. Written texts may present themselves as puzzles that particular readers may solve by drawing upon sense-making practices they have developed in relation to other activities. McHoul calls this particularity "branching" away from any sort of step-by-step process of reading that may be "intended" by the text. McHoul answers text analysts who are always looking for the "right" reading in the conclusion to his book:

> The reader takes his [*sic*] ability to construct a methodical/ rational reading as evidence for the text's methodical/ rational construction. And he takes this construction as not simply "for me" but as open to public view. . . . [H]ermeneutics' thesis of readerly passivity, the view that "understanding is like a process that happens to us" is a radical and ironic underestimation of the mutual and reflexive constitution of reading situations by texts and their readers.[25]

McHoul extends the analysis of texts into the exploration of the cognitive processes involved in reading. This goes beyond the arguments for reading and writing as being no more than legitimating strategies for social institutions. McHoul has made two discoveries that are important to the present inquiry. The first is that reading requires curiosity. The possibility that there is new information on the page presents a challenge that may either serve to reinforce or change the reader's mind. A text may frustrate readers if its meaning is exclusive, that is, if the writing is unreadable to all but certain specialists. Second, reading also requires openness. To be open is to make oneself vulnerable because reading involves positioning. Reading strategies include defensive postures (for example, reading as debate), the desire to give presence to meaning (reading to open the text and to unmask oneself), and the shame involved if one takes a writer's confusion to be one's own. This vulnerability can be employed so as either to express or suppress one's passion.

Writing is more than content formulated as information or abstract matter. It is a creation in time and space re-created as reading-events by living bodies. In this context, readers are more than commodities or receptacles. Actual readers bring physical, intellectual, and emotional lives to bear upon meaning-symbols. These symbols emerge in a telling-act as questions, not as answers. The act of reading is not so much decoding as it is a reaching out with eyes and ears to caress and enliven words, to make them present through imagery — to give them shape. And the form that a reader may give to words is the product of a process of projection.

Reading, Writing, Projection

No reading takes place without comprehension. Comprehension requires perception, matching, and guesswork. Eyes scan a page, focussing on what seems familiar. What is recognized is compared and matched with what the reader already knows. But the match is rarely exact; hence imaginative connections or guesses are required in order for the reader to include her/his understanding in what seems familiar on the page. All three of these phases in reading occur rapidly and interdependently. The various connections between the facets of the reader's work and the page involve complex and highly creative moves on the part of an active reader. Eye movements involved in reading a page have also been studied in depth.

> Instead of gliding smoothly across the text, the eyes jump sharply from one position to another and they remain relatively stationary in each position for about a quarter of a second. These rapid eye movements are referred to as saccades or saccadic movements and the intervening pauses are known as fixations.[26]

The words or phrases apprehended during intervals of fixation require interpretation. Cognitive theorists believe that the meanings seen (or heard) are compared, after a process of sifting and matching through short- and long-term eidetic memory banks, with a kind of subjective lexicon. "According to this view, the reader's task is to use the visual representation of the word to locate the appropriate lexical entry in his [*sic*] mental dictionary."[27]

Yet word and phrase comprehension does not make meaning, and certainly does not address issues such as discomfort or pleasure with a text, as explored by Roland Barthes.[28] Meaning-making requires the ability to form propositions, and to address a text with questions — to address a text as a question. This requires an investment of emotion in the act of reading. Reading can be a way to come to know one's passion. What is written can be taken up in the search for insight. Even a writing about facts can be read for questions. To turn a fact into a question is an inside-out procedure characteristic of reading as weaving, with the use of the eyes as a loom to blend and contrast the known, the desire to know, and the unknown.

> Research based on memory techniques suggests that in comprehending a passage of prose readers construct the individual propositions expressed in the text and combine them to form an organized representation of the material. At some point (or points) in the process they tend to introduce information that is not expressed directly in the text.[29]

Comprehension involves matching. But matching personal images and memories with information on a page is much more than a mechanistic process of sorting and classifying. It requires guessing, and guesswork involves the imagination. Making a text memorable, that is, convivial and thus meaningful, requires a commitment to one's reading as a significant activity. Reading is taking the risk of responding. Every act of reading is an interpretive one, not just of the inscribed signifieds, but also of readerly affect, which leads educator David Bleich to conclude that "the role of personality in response is the most fundamental fact of criticism."[30]

Even the most anonymous of writings can be read imaginatively. Bruno Bettelheim (among others) has referred to active, creative reading as misreading. Misreading is not erroneous reading; neither is it a rare occurrence. It is part of what can happen when one reads something interesting or moving. The more actively a particular reader has engaged the moving text, the more likely (s)he may misread even to the point of reading one word as another. Also, misreading is not sequential. Unrestrained eye movement can release the reader from parochially over-determined, linear ways of reading that suppress saccadic eye movement. Reading then becomes less legalistic, because the unique facticity of the reader participates in the creation of meaning. The text is embraced and projected upon simultaneously.

> In responding to the text, the reader digests some of its meaning in an individual and sometimes idiosyncratic manner. Piaget's concept of assimilation describes well the tendency to make the text's content meaningful according to what the individual thinks he [sic] knows or what he feels. While often the content and what the reader makes of it seem far apart, upon scrutiny a connection can always be found. A misreading thus represents the person's response to the text and his attempt to communicate this response to himself, to the author, or to anybody listening.[31]

The attempt to match text and response is like the weaving of cloth. The reader reaches out to grasp the text's meaning-threads, at the same time sending out a projective thread, a symbol created in her/his imagination that has been stimulated by reading, and which seeks to attach itself to what has been read. This projective thread is fundamental to an active reader's response. "The more intent a reader is on taking in the meaning, the more active he is in his [sic] reading."[32] It is much more difficult to exclude one's life experience from the act of reading than to include it.

Nevertheless, educators are highly skilled at teaching young readers prescribed formulas by which to "get at" meaning and identify structure. Only codified responses are deemed correct, while alternative responses are devalued. Alternate responses, however, are those that make reading at all possible and worth doing, and they may in fact be a form of resistance to reified ways of knowing. The imagination can be very helpful in attempting to make sense of perplexing situations in reality. To fight for multiple creative interpretations is to defend one's passion, a critical capacity not valued by conventional pedagogy.

What makes a text analyst different from a naive reader? Perhaps only the degree of awareness of one's abilities to read and misread. I believe that it is possible for all readers to know about both skills. The following contextural analysis comprises a double reading of a text. It follows two textual/ textural surfaces of the writing — the policy surface: the formal, technical, or correct reading; and an allegorical surface: imaginative, emblematic, fictive, and gestural. This kind of "double" reading is similar to what has been referred to by cognitive theorists as "parallel processing," in which "the subprocesses of reading operate in parallel and interact with one another."[33]

Literary Theory's Contribution

"Parallel processing" is a term in cognitive theory related to a process which literary theorist Mikhail Bakhtin called dialogism. Bakhtin used the terms "hearing" and "voicing" to describe the ways in which writers and readers project a magical vitality into words so that they seem to speak through a naming strategy known as characterization. To characterize is to identify and name in writing personalities and descriptions that hold the potential for reading as a dialogue:

> A character's self-consciousness . . . is thoroughly dialogized: in its every aspect it is turned outward, intensely addressing itself, another, a third person. Outside this living addressivity toward itself and toward the other it does not exist, even for itself.[34]

Bakhtin equated coming-to-know with existence. The desire to know fuels the urge to speak and to listen. The ways in which intentionality can become subverted produces a kind of reading that sometimes does not authentically "listen to" what one knows. This occurs if a reader reifies writing, and approaches the text as a formal and closed object that is capable of sustaining only a sequential and anonymous reading position. For Bakhtin, resistance to objectification allows the reader to maintain the ability to listen and to address. Speaking of Dostoyevsky's writing and why it is so powerful and inspiring to readers, he stated that, "there is nothing merely thing-like, no mere matter, no object — there are only subjects. Therefore there is no word-judgement, no word about an object, no secondhand referential word — there is only the word as address, the word dialogically contacting another word."[35]

> Dialogue here is not the threshold to action; it is a form of action. It is not a means for revealing, for bringing to the surface the already-made of a person; no, in dialogue a person not only shows himself [sic] outwardly, but he becomes for the first time that which he is — and, we repeat, not only for others but for himself as well. To be means to communicate dialogically. When dialogue ends, everything ends.[36]

If to dialogue is to live, is all dialogue alive? It may be created as communication; but may not certain dialogues be more life-giving, more life-affirming than others? Here lies the problem of community. How is there to be sharing in a polyphony of interpretations, which mix styles and genres of writing in a creative search for ways to resist alienation? One path of resistance can be created by reading as the gathering and weaving of threads.

Norman Holland's research has lead him to assert that readers use the written form to reinforce and nurture their identities. In both *Poems in Persons* and *5 Readers Reading*, he has written of four principles which he has seen active in reading: (1) "Each reader tries to compose from the elements of the work a match to his [sic] own characteristic style." He speaks of the experience of having had students describe writers and/or their characterizations as being pained, or cynical, self-indulgent, or adolescent. A reader who persists in reading does so because (s)he can find a way to make sense of what is on the page in relation to her/his own experience of the world. (2) Writers and/or characters must be able to reflect a perspective which the reader would either agree with or oppose — there must be a significant degree of resonance. In other words, a writing must be adaptable to a reader's projections, or to what Holland calls a reader's "defences." Holland would assert that resonance is achieved by an active reader who desires to make sense of all texts in

terms of her/his specific neuroses. (3) Texts that can be
included by a reader's projections are employed to "create a
fantasy of the type that matters to him." Holland assumes
that projecting upon texts is a function of neurosis, and that
reading can act as a creative type of therapy for readers, particularly for students who must share and defend their interpretations in the context of seminar discussions. (4) The projected fantasy is assisted by the text to develop toward a
moral, aesthetic, or intellectual "'point' that enables him
[*sic*] to find in the work unity, significance and pleasure."[37]
The articulation of what has been projected upon the page by
an assemblage of readers is, for Holland, a non-threatening
way of disclosing disquieting emotions which emerge from
deep-seated inner conflicts. Holland is a professor of English,
and he deems his studies to be experiments in the psychoanalysis of literature. He writes not only of personal neurotic
conflict, but also of collective meaning as consisting of the
channelling of personal unconscious movements toward a
common goal, whereby "entire nations transform fantasies
into immense actions and styles."[38] This interpretation
would assume that any national sentiment could be crystal-
lized by a charismatic leader, one who could tap into the
unconscious mechanisms of citizens. While such a view is
thought-provoking, I find Holland's view of reading extreme
and one-sided. He believes that any theory which implies
textual authority is totally misguided. He states that: "It is
not the book that absorbs us; it is we who absorb the book."[39]

Holland has been confined by his research method. To
say that there is something real or vital in the written is to
project attributes onto writing that are not solely the property of the reader. In this view, only the reader's emotions
are currency, and documents have no power. The use of a
method which does not recognize or acknowledge the nego-
tiative features of reading cannot adequately investigate
written perspectives and attitudes, albeit in potential; as
such, Holland saves the reader but slays the text. "The work
finds its fulfillment, so to speak, when a reader gives it life
by re-creating the work in his [*sic*] own mind. The text as
such almost vanishes in the astonishing variability of different readers' re-creations of it."[40]

Textual theorists often favour one side or the other; either the text dominates the reader, or the reader battles to overcome the written. Literary scholar Stanley Fish has suggested that written statements can be active strategies that work upon readers, instead of acting as containers from which any and all kinds of messages may be extracted. In *Is There a Text in This Class? The Authority of Interpretive Communities*, Fish deals predominantly with the anxieties he takes to be fundamental to all reading practices. The written is forever unfolding in the events of reading. Readers, he posits, search for an argument; but the search is never resolved by the text. It is merely intensified. This notion is of foremost interest to him. "In the analysis of a reading experience, when does one come to the point? The answer is never, or no sooner than the pressure to do so becomes unbearable. . . . Coming to the point should be resisted."[41]

Fish insists that his investigations have neither followed nor developed what could be called a method. He has instead found what he takes to be a language-sensitizing device for readers. Each reader's interpretations seek to heighten, then resolve, ambivalence, working for the most part with a host of already available interpretive strategies. For "there is never a moment when one believes nothing, when consciousness is innocent of any and all categories of thought, and whatever categories of thought are operative at a given moment will serve as an undoubted ground."[42] Stanley Fish, in the end, cynically describes some of the implications of institutional authority on reading and writing. His notion of a game swallows up the reading subject. Every member of society is playing this game; culture and members are constituted by the nature of their participation, since "there are no moves that are not moves in the game, and this includes even the move by which one claims no longer to be a player."[43]

Both Holland and Fish have made important contributions to reading theory. Fish has reminded text analysts that the ways in which one is a social player also influence how one reads. Fantasies and other non-verbal patterns, or what Holland calls ego-defences, must be examined in order to develop a more comprehensive view of the operations performed when one is reading. Fish does not situate interpretive acts as being the work of readers; these are the products of rigid cultural categories of thought, whereas Holland places cultural dynamics in the context of a social unconscious.

Ethnography on Shifting Ground

Some anthropologists have discussed figure and ground in relation to cultural textuality/texturality. Robert Brain, in his book *The Decorated Body*, discusses the body as a series of archaeological surfaces that reflect cultural markings:

> The body is a clay to be remodelled and a canvas to be redecorated. Sometimes the results seem to us grotesque; sometimes beautiful. Usually there is some recognizable motive behind body art which we at least half recognize. Even in the West the ghosts of primitive instincts haunt body decoration.[44]

Edmund Leach has talked on the subject of medieval illumination in the text known as the *St. Albans Psalter*. The particular drawing which has excited his interest has two surfaces. It represents the baptism of Christ and consists primarily of two angels and Christ wrapped in a shroud, replete with fish. On one surface, the illuminator has indicated that Christ is the ground and his shroud forms the figure. But from another perspective Christ is the figure and his cloak, now appearing to be more like a skin than a garment, is the ground. Leach analyzes the shifting cloak psychoanalytically, historically, and structurally — as a fish.

> I have been trying to display to you in verbal and visual images the way that medieval Christians made typological transformations from the physical to the metaphysical. . . . We know for certain that the artists of the *St. Albans Psalter* made a close association between fish and the body of Christ.[45]

Leach's anthropological knowledge of cultural transformation through mythological symbolism is here extended to a study of medieval painting, which appears to him to be both representational and allegorical. In other words, it appears to have meaning-content which can be adapted to either of two frames of reference. Both figure and ground move within wide parameters of perception.

Stephen Tyler has adapted a post-structural conceptualization of the intertext to a study of the context of ethnography. In his article, "Ethnography, Intertextuality and the End of Description," he has observed that ethnography's

> representation of native life gives the appearance of a direct confrontation of mind and nature, word and thing, subject and object, of clear referential meaning. This appearance of objectivity seems to deny intertextuality. . . . It indexes an ideological interest in setting literature aside by concealing the artifice that produces the appearance of objectivity.[46]

The "artifice" is the discourse of science, which is inherently textual by virtue of the ways in which both method and theory are produced — as texts in reference to other texts. He calls for the end of ethnographic description as a method, determining that the synthesizing of interpretations pretends to do much to help readers "understand" strangers. Ethnographic formulas are estranged because the writing of recognizable ethnography is based upon a principle of comparative sameness. The differences between "us" and "them" are obscured and devalued. The rituals associated with the writing of ethnographic description, however, carry within them a fundamental "allegorizing identity." This means that there is more possible in ethnography than the reproduction of methodic formulas. For this reason Tyler can attempt in ethnography

> another kind of intertextuality whose project is not to reveal the other in univocal descriptions which allegorically identify the other's difference as our interest. It must be instead a fantasy of identities, a plurivocal evocation of difference that mimics on every page the rationalism that seems to inform it and that reveals between every line the difference it conceals in every word.[47]

Methods of writing that carry an allegorizing potential are those which also generate the notion of an intertext. When allegory is produced in a reading performance, it

means that the reader is dealing with a text that is rhetorical. According to Vincent Leitch's theory, allegorical readings
are "inevitable (mis)readings" — inevitable because the project of an accurate reading is considered impossible:

> When a text is densely rhetorical, it will generate numer-
> ous misreadings. Any critical reading that tries to contain
> the inevitable misreadings itself affirms the inevitability of
> misreading in spite of its very desire to circumscribe the
> random play of grammatical structures and the dizzying
> aberrations of rhetorical figures.[48]

Deconstruction theorists believe, for example, that historical writing is fiction, since reading can only ever produce fictional forms, and all writing requires and incorporates reading. And there are many versions of the same events. By virtue of the debates over what to select and how to present
characters and situations, the lives of our predecessors have
been victimized by historical writing. Acknowledging the
inevitability of fiction has brought deconstruction theorists
to bold reading strategies. "To read closely in the deconstructive or disfigurative manner produces more reliable history
than the history of historicists and archaeologists, who
champion carefully forged lies of order and continuity."[49]

Institutionalized writing promotes the right reading as a
ritual to secure a form of order; this ritual also attempts to
obscure critical struggles to know. Deconstruction theorist
Jacques Derrida brings lying to the attention of readers and
writers. He is sensitive to the rituals of giving an oath as an
interesting site for lies, and is particularly interested in the
signing of one's name as a form of oath. Meditation on the
signature as a problem leads him to discover the umbilicus.
Mother-speech emerges, one could say, from within, but it
cannot be heard if the reader is preoccupied, distracted, or
even intimidated by the Father-pen.

Anonymous writing tries to seduce readers into compul-
sive rituals, offering ready-made regulations as efficient and
comforting answers. By participating in such rituals without
reflecting, reading subjects would drown their curiosity, their
intense interest — a passionate ignorance — the greatest gift
anyone could give to a community. The particular and self-
conscious gift of a reader's ignorance cannot be accepted

when it is not recognized as significant. To admit one's ignorance is a form of treason if the state asserts that it provides all that is essential to be known. Socrates may be said to have been put to death for teaching too well, for making people curious. To call taken-for-granted "social knowledge" into question is to read/weave gesturally. To then analyze the texture of one's reading is to give a gift when a tax is requested — the tax of a national/federal oath. Oath as a tax requires that one feel like a responsible citizen who pays one's tax through reading as self-sacrifice and the denial of one's own body (which retains scars of kinship) in the interest of the state's body of knowledge.

3 Confederation and the Body of Conflict

A lthough Chapter One indicates that the Task Force was composed of "eight Canadian men and women," the production of the *Report of the Task Force on Canadian Unity* included many more people. The *Report* had a mandate, which assumed a "public," addressed and edited by the panel of eight, who were by no means all of the "members" of the Task Force. The staff that advised, co-ordinated, and wrote the three volumes of this *Report* included 165 people. This effectively created an anonymous author composed of multiple, supplemental authors. No one wrote these documents. They were generated by a small army of federal government employees. As Michel Foucault concluded in his article "What Is an Author?"

> It does not seem necessary that the author-function remain constant in form, complexity, and even in existence. I think that, as our society changes, at the very moment when it is in the process of changing, the author-function will disappear.[50]

One way in which the author-function evaporates is by imitation. In federal documents, the work of writing becomes the work of reproducing a Canadian style; some of the assumptions involved in this style are outlined in the federally published book *The Canadian Style*. One chapter pertains to "Reports and Minutes," which, when constructing the "body" of any report, advises the "author" to describe "the purpose, method and other circumstances of the activity being reported on (the introduction); the conduct of the

---

Notes to Chapter 3 are on pp. 114-16.

experiment or other activity (the report proper); and the results, recommendations and comments (the conclusion)."[51]

The Canadian style of report writing prescribes that the writing must focus on some activity and that a method will be employed to acknowledge that activity as a type of conduct worthy of research. "Method" here refers to propositions which attempt to persuade the reader that the writing should be judged as worthy. If worthiness is granted, then the written activity will become a reportable event. The method will be recognized more readily (after the fact, as a "circumstance of the activity" being written about as a way to make it look identifiably scientific) if an "experiment" can be shown to have been conducted. Further, the full shape of the "body" can be identified once the findings of the experiment have been articulated as results that are regarded as useful (being capable of re-use) when recommendations can be provided. Following recommendations means that an attempt can be made to reproduce the object of the experiment through principles that indicate how to appropriately attend to the activity-*cum*-event-*cum*-object, and/or how to replicate an empirical method by making claims that both address and report in an experimental style. The researcher, as writer, collapses discovery and analysis into one processed conclusion and thus becomes anonymous, as a direct result of her/his imitative method.

Method can be imitative, and that imitation can become confused with the formatting and writing style from which it was derived to such a degree that the imitation can be mistaken as a possible site for development and even discovery. This crisis in method is far from chaotic. One way to understand it is to observe what method excludes in many forms of writing, be they fictional, federal, or sociological. Discovery in science, for example, is only discovery when the procedures have been documented, articulated in an appropriate written form, and replicated. The results need not be consistent in the replication of an experiment. As long as the same procedures have been followed then even inconsistent results can be published.[52]

In the case of commissions, special committees of inquiry, and task forces, the imitation of a federal style is so well

honed that personal critical reflection is not considered significant to the findings and is therefore procedurally disal-
lowed. According to correct procedure, an individual viewpoint could be construed as a non-objective "bias," an unpro-
fessional attitude towards the research at hand which, in the
case under consideration here, involves travelling across
Canada, listening to people discuss a variety of topics, and
then offering advice after collecting data (i.e., people's comments). The agenda is, however, defined in advance by those
funding and instigating the research. In the case of this *Task
Force Report*, "crisis" was recognized in Ottawa as something
requiring definition and remedy through research. The
Report uses an official "we," represented by the jury of eight
who conducted the hearings, and who received their data
from eyes that saw and ears that heard. The eight "we"
employed their hearings so as to fulfill their mandate, and
subsequently their researchers adapted the data (what was
heard) for the purpose of providing recommendations on
something already deemed a "crisis." This crisis and its remedy were not discovered by anyone from among the team of
researchers/writers/diagnosticians. They were hired to find
and mend the source(s) of conflict, with "mend" here meaning the proposal of policy solutions in writing as the best
remedy for the crisis, an originary and threatening force.

An "Agenda for Change"

Chapter One is named "Agenda for Change." The word
agenda in this title connotes committee meetings, in which
discussion pinpoints problems and requires that solutions be
found in an efficient way. "The Task Force on Canadian
Unity was created on 5 July 1977" to seek and make public
citizens' opinions on Canada and to share in return "the
ideas and initiatives of the members of the Task Force on the
question of Canadian Unity."[53] The opening chapter promises an agenda in its title; and the justification for an agenda
precedes any details of one.

> Canada and its constitutional system is in a protracted
> state of crisis; the primary, but not the only challenge,
> comes from Quebec; and the pressing need today, as it was
> then, is to discover the basis for a fresh accommodation
> which will permit the people who inhabit this vexing and
> marvellous country to live together in peace, harmony and
> liberty.[54]

The agenda is required because Quebec has presented a
"challenge" to the confederate body — by presenting itself as
another body. The agenda will propose measures to bring
about peace and harmony before/as liberty; however, there is
no mention of equality or reciprocity.

Thomas Hobbes, as proto-sociologist, and Auguste Comte,
recognized as one of the first sociologists, both wrote about
the state as a body — as a Leviathan and as the supreme
being "Humanity," respectively.[55] Although writing in different times and places, both of these theorists were primarily
concerned with order in the interest of securing long-lasting
"health" for the entire body of the state that was constructed
as a single, anonymous unit. As has been suggested in the
work of Dorothy Smith, this positivistic unit is first and foremost recognizable for the writing which it generates.[56]

There are further clues as to the orientation of the
agenda, which relate to public policy. Report writers have
attempted to anticipate reading questions that they consider
fundamental to the articulation of their agenda. Thus, in
anticipation of the question, "Why promote unity via public
policy?" four replies are provided. First, public attitudes are
more likely to change if institutions change first. Second, the
reader is told that individual attitudes cannot be changed by
reports. Third, the crisis of Confederation requires immediate response, and governments are described as being able to
respond more quickly to crises than can small groups.
Fourth, it is stated that individuals across the country have
told Task Force researchers that they as citizens expect
changes on the level of "political and institutional reform."

The *Report* articulates itself as a policy threshold. This
use of the word "threshold" comes from Mikhail Bakhtin's
discovery of a form of writing that perpetuates tensions that

can develop into crises designed to develop characters and to bring them toward insight. The ability to create and perpetuate a crisis through writing thus comes to constitute a stylistic gesture. To read further is to find out more about a crisis. The Task Force agenda will write a crisis and its diagnosis, explaining what is wrong with the confederation's body, not only in the provinces and regions, but also in the attitudes of citizens who have spoken out. The *Report* will remain a "dialogue on the threshold"[57] throughout, since what will be diagnosed and prescribed will not be implemented by this writing. The *Report* writers make recommendations which they have no power to implement.

The writers hoped that the *Report* would act both as a catalyst to policy and as a potential influence on the attitudes of citizens, which were assessed and re-articulated as various forms of help or hindrance in the crisis. "Selfish" citizens who spoke before the Task Force commissioners across the country provided what is described as "analysis," that is, any reading of Canada which attends to policy inadequacies, and which acknowledges many different persons, not just one "we." This may be called selfish because selves are made uncomfortably present to anonymity by this process. As one citizen commented, "It is obvious that the federal system, as we have known it up until now, does not . . . provide for a dialogue where both linguistic groups have sufficient confidence in the fairness of the structure and the equality of representation."[58]

Instead of supposedly disruptive critical analyses, unselfish patriots offered a form of "diagnosis," while patriots were identified as those "whose concern transparently was not with self but with country."[59] Worry about the confederate body was identified as a link to connect citizens with the aims of Task Force writers. "Unselfish" concern about the country qualified citizens to join the enclave of diagnosticians, to stand in their midst as apprentices in the method of diagnosing federally perceived social organisms, and as cadets in the war against critical analyses. The concern of potential diagnosticians, as new patriots, needs to be deepened and sharpened in a particular way; citizens must stop doing selfish analyses. Analysis is defined as a myopic concern, as the cause of confusion and fragmentation across the country. It is given as the reason for citizen unrest, and is equated with "diversity in ignorance of itself." Analysis produces ignorance because it is defined in the *Report* as a way of thinking based on self-involvement and isolation. Analysis, synonymous with misguided meaning and solipsistic concerns, is to be avoided. New patriots must strive to be compassionate, and to "cherish and embrace diversity."[60] The embrace to be learned is the one that would engulf and contain diversity. Communities, no longer analyzing in isolation, will be counted and reproduced as identifiable federal units.

The *Report* can be said to constitute a diagnostic manual for learning the essential discursive strategies of new patriotism. A patriot is one who understands that unity has never really existed in Canada. Confederation has been a wish, a pretence by which it was hoped that diverse groups of citizens might agree to unite as a "harmonious combination of parts."[61]

Chapter One concludes by having developed something of the moral dimension of the crisis as harboured by isolated pockets of citizens whose "analysis" prevents them from becoming new patriots. In the view of a government committee anxious for unity, a crisis signals a state that has lost control. According to federal report writers, one social body, namely "Confederation" has lost this control. Any older shreds of patriotism have been eroded by such things as "suspicion and occasional hostility, envy, intolerance and parochialism."[62] These reactions are believed to have caused the confederate body to become weaker and weaker; it was destroyed by the forfeited realization of its wish. A change in attitude is required by all; the orientation towards the ability to "cherish and embrace" would constitute a significant step towards the health of the social body as it is described in this *Report*. But before there can be any change in attitude, an attitude problem must be stated and acknowledged, as must the crisis in which it participates. Citizens who can face their attitude problems and can acknowledge the crisis in the terms of the Task Force are deemed eligible to join the diagnosticians, and these persons will become new patriots, citizens anxious to aid in the development of a fresh unity as components of a healthier, more efficient Canada.

Citizens must acquire more "staying power." The power to stay is the power to relearn and remember the importance of particular events to the life of Canada. Staying is the redevelopment of a common thought-project that involves the selection of specific events as important, and the agreement of the community of Canadians on the importance of these events as significant in Canadian history, until such time as citizens might be asked to alter or shift their focus to another federal formulation. The event that Chapter Two asks citizens to remember occurred in 1976: "The point of departure for the Task Force cannot be other than the election of the Parti Quebecois as the government of Quebec on 15 November," which "should be taken to symbolize the political crisis Canada is facing, rather than to constitute it."[63] Another historically significant event, relating to the political crisis, was the publication of the findings of *The B & B Commission*, which is identified as the prophet or herald of the Task Force's crisis, having described resentment between French and English Canadians as already deeply entrenched in the 1960s. *B & B* researchers predicted that the crisis would get worse unless sincere and far-ranging steps were taken to overcome it. The remedies administered to the confederate body in the 1960s and 1970s included the *Official Languages Act* of 1969, the bilingual self-declaration by the province of New Brunswick, expanded French-language educational programs in Ontario, and the regulation of the language of work in Quebec with Bills 22 and 101.[64]

These measures, however, were not enough to rid the social body of resentment. *B & B's* proposed remedies "produced a backlash in English-speaking Canada which in turn generated a reverse effect in Quebec."[65] This "reverse effect," including such events as the air traffic controllers' strike, is identified as having a direct correlation with the PQ victory. One message underlying this chapter of the *Report* is that *B & B* had powerful effects on the course of modern Canadian history. Although it produced effects that were later taken to be the "reverse" of those initially hoped for, this commission's report has nonetheless been given weight in terms of its influence on the 10 years of political history that followed its findings and recommendations. This communicates to citizens that government research has political impact and should be heeded, especially when it provides compelling evidence, as Chua has shown.

Government research reports are not only powerful because they inform policy, and even perhaps, as is suggested by the Task Force, backlashes, elections, and strikes. These reports also perform a vital pedagogical function, instructing politicians, business people, and the general public about worldwide economic patterns, technological advances, and the ways in which Canada is viewed by and relates to the rest of the world. The message here is that Ottawa bears responsibility for "Canada as a whole" as a country within a larger network — the world as a collection of countries which maintain a delicate balance through speculative interactions. For the sake of maintaining an arbitrary world order, each portion of Canada is represented by the federal government in its relations with the rest of the world (whether or not these portions wish to be so represented).

Quebecois who support the PQ are described as seriously misguided citizens (who nonetheless have the potential to become new patriots) because they have turned to Quebec rather than to Ottawa with their concerns. The implication is that they have looked to straw men for leadership in a time when only leaders who have the widest reaching perspective can be helpful. These "misguided" citizens do not realize that their anxieties and worries, described in Chapter Two as having arisen mainly from modernization, are also being experienced by other Canadians and by people in other countries. The implicit formulation is that worldwide change shows that Quebec's actions are uninformed reactions.[66]

The description revolves around European economic history. Economic alliances, culminating in the Common Market, produced regional discontent in various parts of Europe. The reaccentuation of the many and particular peoples and cultures which constitute Europe inspired Quebec's desire for automony. Quebec's reaction in turn re-stimulated regional sentiments elsewhere in Canada that "had remained relatively muted between the Second World War and the 1960s. . . . The revival of regionalism was assisted by Quebec. . . . The crisis which the country faces today is not one of

Quebec or French Canada only: it is a crisis of Confederation itself."[67]

Quebec is described as having assisted in bringing about the crisis at hand. Its responsibility is further muted by international events, and its struggle for autonomy, as a force to affect and inspire others, is downplayed as being just one of many factors. Nonetheless, Quebec, however unwittingly, emerges as the villain of the *Report*, having introduced a body of actions and ideas that conflicts with the confederate body. This body of conflict attracts citizens without staying power who succumb to short-sighted "analyses" due to their neglect (a Task Force term used to describe the situation of the native peoples), vulnerability (which refers specifically to the condition of the Canadian economy), and "little loyalty" (understood federally as "the growing cynicism of many citizens towards a bureaucracy which they wrongly perceive to be withholding and distant").[68]

The body of Unity as called for by this document is said to have never before existed; patriots were participants in a rough-and-ready consensus that was strong enough to pull through other crises, but not this one. The new patriot would resist the temptation to ignore the neglected. (S)he would be strong, and would not be swayed from her/his allegiance by some vague "unfair stereotype" that seems to equate the hard-working government with "a remote shambling bureaucracy that exacts tribute from its subjects and gives little in return."[69] Citizenship must now become self-conscious in order to construct the new Unity body. True citizens are those who will not "doubt" their country. Doubt is seen to have emerged from doing isolated forms of "analysis" in a time of global anxiety, and, by seeking advice from, or from having become enthralled by, Quebec.

Reading "The Anatomy of Conflict"

Chapter Three of the *Report*, "The Anatomy of Conflict," implies that the source of the crisis is external to, and of an anatomy other than, the confederate social body. Analogically, the contractually organized geographic anatomy is in conflict with another organism (referred to as a purveyor of conflict) that this chapter promises to dissect. In the second chapter, a distinction was made between the people of Quebec and the PQ. The people of Quebec turned to their provincial government out of great anxiety, and the *Task Force Report* states that they were misled into thinking about independence by very strange leaders, whose views were destructive to Canada (in both its old and new versions). People from other regions are shown to be looking to Quebec as an example of a group fighting for autonomy. These citizens are described as misguided in thinking that Ottawa does not respect, and cannot accommodate, concerns unique to their communities.

The Task Force states that it acknowledges regional concerns, not solipsistic ones. The difference seems to lie once again in a written description of attitudes. A patriotic regionalist faces the so-called realities of changing international history, while a self-indulgent citizen listens to those who preach self-sufficiency that ultimately spells economic isolation and ostracism from federal protection. The head of this isolating body of conflict is the PQ, which is at the centre of the present crisis. Having not only excited regionalists again, the PQ has also supposedly stirred up natives and ethnic groups, such that these groups must also somehow be appeased, accommodated, and at the same time brought into line by a federal unity policy.[70]

The confederate body was founded upon dualism, as was legally formulated in the *BNA Act*. This body was later sustained by a number of more complex formulations that emerged from the original definition of dualism, and included theories about two founding peoples, in a country with two different languages, and of two nations. But this dual status was capable of being maintained only as long as it was an agreement between groups of people who understood each other's circumstances.

Edmund Leach posits the notion that most relationships, either domestic or professional, are of what he calls the "asymmetrical hierarchical" type. The forms of relation that differ from this (or at least make a conscious effort to), are those of friends who struggle for symmetrical equality and emphasize their commonalities; and of enemies, who struggle for a symmetrically balanced form of inequality that always emphasizes points of disagreement. Enemies can trust in their disagreements as predictable and regulating features of their relations. As such, one can predict the actions of long-time superiors, friends, and of known enemies. The most radical of relations are those developed with strangers, whose actions seem thoroughly unpredictable and generally incomprehensible. Leach, in *Social Anthropology*, explains that

> When we quarrel with potential friends, we still recognize them as "people like us," both sides will conform to the same rules of the game. In sharp contrast, in wars of conquest and extermination against total strangers, there are no rules of the game. Strangers do not rate as human beings at all. . . . This . . . illusion is directly linked to the universal belief that "we" (people like us) can be distinguished from "they" (people who are like us in external form but not like us in their inner essence).[71]

Leach then alludes to the importance of mytho-history, the tales of origin that continually construct and reinforce the us/they distinctions. In the case of the *Task Force Report*, the mytho-history is being rewritten as an allegory. Quebec's change of orientation has had regional, ethnic, and native repercussions that have resounded like shock waves throughout the confederate body. The resonating effects of the PQ alien force were to be distanced from Canada's body by being articulated as a separate mythical being, a body of conflict.

Chapter Three postulates many factors contributing to the so-called profound changes in Quebec's perceptions of itself and of Canada. Ethnic and geographic history, language, and the legal system are outlined. One concept that is highlighted is Quebec's change in cultural theme, from one of *survivance* (survival) to one of *épanouissement* (blossoming into self-fulfillment).[72] Survival is a mythological theme that has been employed to maintain connections between diverse groups throughout both the United States and Canada. The US calls its survivors "pioneers"; Canada calls them "settlers." These were the "rough and ready" who stuck together

and could survive just about anything—anything except
what might occur if they could no longer communicate, having gone their separate ways.

There is an air of indignation in the *Task Force Report*
about one province deciding to change its mythology, to
re-orient its identity to one of "blossoming" when the rest of
the country (other groups within Canada not inspired to
think autonomously) is still thinking in terms of the prescribed survival theme. This independent identity shift has
become understood in the context of the *Report* as the birth
of a new body, the body of conflict. In federal terms, two
social bodies cannot be autonomously vital and burgeoning
in one country at the same time. If the conflict body, as the
"interplay of duality and regionalism" is growing and gaining
strength, then the confederate body must be dying. In the
perspective of Task Force researchers writing on history as
social bodies, Canada was a culture "knit together in defiance of geography"[73] with the help of a single mytho-history
of survival: a logic of necessity, in contrast to blossoming,
which is a carnivalesque logic of fertility.

Another important aspect of the conflict in mythologies is
that French-Canadians (in common with many other immi-
grant and native peoples) has always maintained an oral culture, while English-Canada has been a culture of writing.
Derrida, in *Otobiographies*, indicates a potential conflict
between *l'oreille* (the ear), which attends to *la langue mater-
nelle* (the mother tongue, one's first language), and *le patro-
nyme*, the surname which is one's inheritance from one's
father. Derrida maintains that lineage by surname is the
inheritance of the logos, the imposition of paternal questions
of truth and essence on writing.[74] Although specifically not
an absolute distinction between oral and written language,
Derrida's formulation nevertheless points out some interesting tensions between these two. Hearing is done with the
ear, and speaking with the mouth. Reading is done with the
eyes, and writing with the hand. Separating the perceptual
organs in this way is indeed arbitrary, but doing so may help
to elucidate the *Report*'s description of citizens who "barely
seemed to hear" one another at the Task Force hearings.
Each interest group listens to a different (local, ethnically

based) mother tongue, and cannot readily relate to the writing of the confederate father figure. Some citizens privilege listening, and others reading. The federal words require attention to a lineage not learned from, nor sustainable by, the mother tongue. A different myth of origin must be sustained; new patriots must adjust their perceptual strategies and become oriented to reading a narrative differently from the mytho-history which they have heard. Policy and technology generate mythologies which must be looked at with the umbilicus (the eyes connected to the pen).

The Task Force asks: "Why is it that we have not learned better to employ this century's communications technology to talk together across the empty spaces?"[75] Yet there is no problem with hearing, as the *Report* elsewhere admits. When native and ethnically differentiated groups wish to listen to what is happening in Quebec, they do so easily. The problem is with "seeing" a federal body of legal documents across a vast space. Print must be close to the eyes in order to be read, and can, of course, travel by cable to and from computer terminals. But the space is not just geographic. A document that travels from Ottawa to a terminal on an Ojibwa reserve will be treated differently by the different readers. They can read the same information but from very different vantage points, depending upon their orientations.

Contractual inscription is not an adequate way of delineating a state's body in order to make it perceptible to listeners. Local and indigenous cultures cannot recognize the written federal father as a distinct figure. He is not a part of their landscape. Furthermore, the landscape is not empty space to them. It is fertile geography: Mother earth (Mother tongue). The documentary social body sees only the space as empty. The Father-document cannot talk to Mother earth: he cannot hear; he can only read. He cannot listen or speak to, touch or taste local cultures. Local interests are then strange to his eyes, the eyes of a deaf-mute that have relentlessly privileged one way of writing; he thinks that everyone else should use their eyes as hands, the way that he does.

> For a start, most Quebecois we observed, are not inclined to see regionalism as a very significant factor in Canadian life; they view Canada essentially in terms of the relations

between French and English-speaking Canadians or between Quebec and the rest of Canada. As a result of this dualistic outlook, they are sometimes tempted to think of English-speaking Canada as one monolithic identity.[76]

The *Task Force Report* reconstructs Canadian history as the fading life of the confederate social body, an icon that supposedly was not monolithic, and which included Quebec. But Quebec is then perceived to have become troublesome in having spontaneously "blossomed" beyond the scope of the federation's gaze; the PQ is blamed for instigating independentist rebellion amongst Quebecois, which, the *Report* asserts, has also stirred up other groups of Canadians. This French-Canadian "dualistic outlook" has been written as a Quebecois invention that was uncovered by the writers of the *B & B Commission. B & B* researchers and writers formally articulated the causes of French dualism in the federal writing style.

The *Task Force Report* was written by policy-writers, members of the federal culture of the pen. Quebec is an oral, locally oriented culture of the ear that hears regionalists and natives, but not as legally written Canadians. Oral and written versions of culture are quite different. Anthropologists and researchers in cognitive and communication studies have struggled long and hard to try to do justice to oral cultures, cognizant of the limitations of social scientific categories. At worst, transcribing cultures of the ear into the written form changes them into sets of legalistic definitions and procedures, not living cultures. Ethnicity, when alive, like all living things, is constantly changing; "given the fluid character of regionalism"[77] it is very difficult for anonymous researchers to grasp. It can be heard, however, in dialects, familial concerns, and local cultural production.

Federal researchers, however, have tried to pin down ethnicity in writing. The Task Force researchers write that they observed the Quebecois, but only in federal terminology. To observe is to attenuate the senses, for anonymous watching and listening are passive. Writing research reports and public policy documents is bureaucratically deemed active, distributive, responsible, of a sharing nature, just, and democratic. The *Report*'s interpretation of the oral/aural body is an attempt to reorder the ear, to bring it within the federal boundaries of the umbilicus (eye-hand-pen) in a discourse of provincial jurisdiction and contractual tradition. Federal description privileges sight for writing while living culture prefers speaking and hearing, not anonymous reading. The anatomy of the oral/aural body is not in conflict with itself. The conflict is a crisis of difference in perceptual orientations, in how perceived insights are to be understood and employed. One example of the problems involved in attempting to communicate in light of major differences occurs even in the *Report*'s efforts to acknowledge and accommodate the many different cultures which come under the judicial canopy of Canada. Report writers assume that Quebec is a monolith, and not replete with difference. In their view, "the regional nature of English-speaking Canada complicates its perception of French-speaking Canada, just as the comparatively homogeneous and concentrated character of Quebec society complicates its perception of the rest of the country."[78] The *Task Force Report* writers focus on this difference—the one between a segmented English-speaking Canada and a monolithic Quebec.

The oral/aural body looks "homogeneous" to federal culture-readers because Quebec's differences have been isolated within a set of provincial boundaries; it has long been cordoned off as an ethnic region with "special concerns." But Task Force writers cannot read Quebec as anything other than homogeneous within its legally assigned boundaries. Because these writers cannot (or will not) hear local cultural production, Quebec's blossoming is read as inappropriate. The researchers do not acknowledge that the limitations of their own interpretive strategies are problematic. Federal discourse, therefore, is limited in its perceptual capabilities, in that it has the ability to interpret within limited parameters by recognizing provinces and provincially determined "regions" as capable of culture. These sites can be seen by federal researchers because they have already been defined as essentially Canadian. The reseachers can only include in their "we" other persons whom they recognize as Canadians, who allow the government style to write "us." They state, "we regard the provincial and territorial governments as critical agents in articulating the concerns and aspirations of these regional communities."[79]

"Critical agents" is a term which refers to the middle-management of the state, crucial for the employment and enforcement of federal terminology and strategies. The description of what is critical is quite different from what sociology would recognize as critical. In his article "Critical Theory and Critical Sociology," Ray Morrow points out that: "given its origins as part of a movement of resistance against fascism and nationalism, critical theory inevitably remains suspicious of nationalism in any guise."[80] The anonymous agency of provincial governments is not critical; "critical agents" are important for policy implementation, for example, for the legal and spacial interpretation of the status of persons.

Any writing, or telling, that potentially subverts subjective presence[81] could be a site for critical inquiry in sociology, which attends to the articulation and restoration of the subject to society, that is, the process of the empowerment of living, acting, creative persons. Critical theorists are suspicious of national interests when, instead of local subjects, organizations for the social body and inscribed constructs that organize persons into provincial and territorial populations take precedence. A call to citizens to donate their perceptual organs to a "we" construction could be implemented through provincial bureaucracies as instructional "critical agents." But critical theory is also critical of "critical agents" who are seen to reproduce a discourse which shames subjects into donating, under the rubric of patriotism. A donation which is not freely given is a form of taxation.

Rewriting *Épanouissement*

It was necessary, in keeping with anonymous style, for the writers of the *Task Force Report* to rewrite local concerns as a body of conflict. This locale had to be transformed; instead of being the many and different interest groups which include French-Canadians, other ethnic minorities, natives, and regionalists, it was (re)written only as one figure, as the social body of an unruly Quebec. Such a writing attempted to contain *épanouissement*, or the blossoming of culture, to stop its "swelling" from spreading. This helps to explain the document's curious return to a narration on dualism, as necessitated by the demands of a fiercely homogeneous, indeed tribal, Quebec which has been traditionally humoured collectively by the "rest" of Canada, always identified as the "English-speaking" who share a "common 'political culture.'"[82] "Common" politics is an agreement about federalism, a commitment to/of provinces to remain confederal. The Task Force's version of Quebec has broken its promise because it will not speak or listen in the federal language. To be dual means to compromise, to share a language in common which should act as a mutually beneficial bridge. The *Task Force Report* states that this bridge has been destroyed by the suggestion of sovereignty-association. The *Report* writers have read the sovereignty-association suggestion as "a refusal to continue to ask and answer the [duality] question at all."[83] Association becomes separation when the concept of duality, with its bridge to unity, is called into question. This swing, from white to black, ally to enemy, occurs when concepts of patriotism privilege oneness. "One country, one flag, one people,"[84] with two nations, two social bodies that could come to be connected "merely" by association, had to be written as the potential end of the state. Since there was no policy precedent for the *Report*'s researchers to fall back on (precedence is a co-ordinating principle at the heart of anonymous research), talk of sovereignty-association from Quebec entered federal perception as automatically voiced utterances intruding on ears that did not expect anything nearly so new and so foreign to tradition/precedent (and hence to regulation) as blossoming. I have coined the term "automatic voicing" as a suture of Bakhtin's concept of voicing in dialogism, the voice being the speaking personality in poetry or prose, in combination with William James's formulation of automatic writing, as a writing which seems to be produced out of nowhere, beyond the conscious control of the writer.[85] I employ automatic voicing in the present case to describe a perplexed reaction within the *Report* to ideas like *épanouissement* that seem to its writers to have appeared spontaneously, as if from out of nowhere, but speaking with definition and strength of purpose.

Chapter Three concludes with a writing of two social bodies as a crisis in Canadian history. New patriots will use this information, based on the international and far-reaching expertise of federal researchers, to diagnose local versions of the crisis "correctly," that is, after having produced a correct reading of a Canada in conflict and split asunder, the only solution is to construct a new Canada out of a new way of thinking about Canada. The rest of the document attends to the writing of this new thinking.

Once the body of conflict was delineated, once Quebec was inscribed as the instigating force behind the crisis in Canadian unity, it then became possible for the *Report* to express concern for this deviant-made-alien and to explore the ways in which "they," the people of Quebec, have had many of the same economic and cultural problems that "we," the citizens of the rest of Canada, have endured. This description gives dualism an inscribed identity. Speaking of sameness is a way of returning to duality by way of equality. "Besides demographic evidence, the principle of duality or dualism is often supported by a number of historical, legal and political concepts such as 'the two founding peoples,' the 'compact theory of Confederation,' 'the two nations,' and 'equal partnership.'"[86] Dualism is arbitrarily related to oneness, and it leaves no room for such concepts as sovereignty-association, which implies the acceptance of multiplicity and as such is a concept that threatens federal unity and thought. The concepts of multiple voicing and equality cannot be accommodated by the Task Force's version/vision of Canadian unity. Thus, association is described as a concept for the confused.

Dualism is the only concept to be thought in relation to equality. The *Report* moves towards a writing of equality by employing interesting stylistic features that are best described as a kind of character development. If one reads the dual "bodies" in a literary manner, one being an alien force blossoming beside an arcane, confederate body, then one can refer to some novelistic precedents for this kind of narrative, the most famous being Dostoyevsky's *The Double*. In that book, Dostoyevsky introduces a character named

Golyadkin, who discovers another separate and distinct personality within himself. Bakhtin elaborates:

> that second voice is to such a degree unable to merge with the first, it feels so threateningly independent, that in place of comforting and encouraging tones there begin to appear teasing, mocking and treacherous ones. With astonishing tact and artistry Dostoyevsky transfers — almost imperceptibly to the reader — Golyadkin's second voice from his interior dialogue to the narration itself: it begins to sound like an outside voice.[87]

Double-characterization develops within Golyadkin as anti-hero when he is unable to be intimate with other persons, and he produces a friend within his own imagination. The second voice is not under the control of the first personality; it is in fact an obnoxious and treacherous co-habitant of Golyadkin's body. As the novel unfolds, the second voice develops a phantom body which Golyadkin sees and relates to as another person. Unfortunately, this fantasy friend proves untrustworthy. The other personality turns against its fashioner and treats him with contempt, making co-habitation with its imaginary being even worse than the indifferent treatment by real persons, which Golyadkin senses. The fantasy-equal becomes Golyadkin's nemesis, particularly when the equal figure himself becomes double-voiced, and is thus doubly mocking (as double and narrator alternately). Bakhtin explains that this double is not a fully developed characterization; the novel is not monologic (single-voiced) nor is it yet polyphonic (many voiced); hence, the almost two voices of he/they whom Dostoyevsky calls Golyadkin Senior and Junior, operate on a rudimentary level of dialogicality. Perhaps it is this rudimentarity which leads Bakhtin to situate *The Double* within the genre of the "morality play, in which the actors are not whole people but rather the spiritual forces battling within them." Here, as elsewhere in his book, *Problems of Dostoyevsky's Poetics*, Bakhtin explains what a "whole" character sounds like in Dostoyevsky's work by assessing the "wholeness" of characters according to the degree of polyphony that any one character can accommodate.[88]

Bakhtin's insights are very helpful in analyzing the two social bodies which have been written into the *Task Force*

Report. Once equal, both become levelled. This levelling emerges within the *Report* as a movement from "we" to "they," and then to a more all-encompassing "we" that absorbs and forgets difference. Alexis de Tocqueville perceived the tendency towards levelling (as dictatorship) in democratic states as a tendency that accompanied the rhetoric of equality. He stated:

> I believe that it is easier to establish an absolute and despotic government among a people whose social conditions are equal than among any other. I also believe that such a government once established in such a people would not only oppress men [*sic*] but would, in the end, strip each man there of several of the chief attributes of humanity.[89]

This suggests that once equality has become defined by the state, once it has become a standard by which the relations of actual persons are weighed and measured, once equality becomes quantified and legitimated, it ceases to allow local persons to be factually present in the production of meaning. The notion of the abstract, anonymous equal devoid of dialogue becomes the occasion for wretchedness. All members gain the right to become equally alienated. Actual subjectivities are equally unrecognizable. All have access to the same standard, the same scale of "justice," a measure based upon indifference and the absence of the possibility of recognizing difference as anything other than alien and potentially hostile.

Human beings become alienated from their society in the writing of state-defined equality, and become discrete units, numbered and indistinct within the body politic. This is one of the most profound differences between indigenous societies and social bodies organized and reproduced through anonymous writing. In the former, no organizational distinction was made between individuals and the interests and identity of the community as a whole (with such communities remaining small enough to maintain intimate relations among all members); in the latter, persons are set apart from the theoretical evaluation and scientific/architectonic production of enormous communities, which reorganize these same persons into members. Members, in this context, re-enter community as an abstracted circumstance. The actual subject becomes a semio-subject, an ordered, re-organized member — a citizen. Citizenship (or patriotism) is an alienating form of membership. In allowing oneself to be reorganized in the state's terms, one is in danger of living out the state's vision at the expense of one's own.

Here again the case of the double comes into play. Golyadkin cannot tell the difference between fantasy and reality. His double comes to act as another person to such a degree that Golyadkin encounters him on occasion in the everyday world. Once produced, Golyadkin forgets that his double is his own creative fiction. He forgets his fantasy, forgetting at the same time that a fantasy cannot have a real body, and thus that it cannot be engaged in conversation in a coffee-house. The fantasy body in this story becomes confused with the written presence of a "real" body. In relation to the construction of the citizen as participant in the reproduction of abstract (fantasy) social bodies, citizens must read and affirm the federal reconstruction of mytho-history as real Canadian history. In this version of history, Quebec is the *Report*'s double. Quebec comes to be written as disorganized, chaotic, and even delirious. Delirium means (formerly, to go out of the furrow when plowing) being in such a condition, a "state" where one's gestures lose their social significance; these become "unable to be read" (de-lire) by diagnosticians.

The writing of a doubling as duality that becomes equal is not to be taken to be alienating because there are "two." The second one is a reaction to something that could not be ignored or forgotten; it is interpreted as intruding from an external realm. This arbitrary internal/external distinction is the basis of doubling whereby an "external" seems to be in conflict with an "internal." The "two" emerge from a context within which there never was fully a "one" to begin with. An entire one would not interpret anxiety as another being. This "less than one" was the body of Confederation, now rewritten. Equalizing the two social bodies involves writing them flat, without unique features, a process that is a corruption of moral equality, a written mutilation. The *Report* suggests that the reader forget what (s)he has read by rewriting the duality it has just explained, making the less than two into a new "one."

4   Writing a Body of Unity: Rewriting "Canada and the Search for Unity"

On "Canada and the Search for Unity"

"Canada and the Search for Unity," Chapter Four of the *Task Force Report*, promotes the idea that the new Canada is neither the arcane confederate body nor the alien instigator, but a new body of "unity," surmounting all conflicts. This chapter looks to the future, in the hope of creating a brand new, stronger, more effective social body for Canada. While striving for unity is advertised as the best solution to the conflict, the history of Canadian unity is presented as a raft of volatile issues that "has bobbed up and down in public consciousness like a cork in a choppy sea."[90] What seems to be bobbing here is federal writing on unity and the discourse that promotes Canadian history as three social bodies. In my reading I will make sense of this volatile writing by following the cork.

The *Report* is attempting to produce its own unity, which is inscribed as the topic of Canada's unity. It also seeks to ground itself by rewriting a history employing many rhetorical narrative strategies found in fiction. Rhetorical gesticulation is the discursive model for the "motions" produced by the Task Force's search for unity, in light of the doubling and recentring attempts of the writing. I use the word rhetoric in the way that Paul de Man employed the term, in reference to textual dynamics. He stated that: "the aphoria between performative and constative language is merely a version of the

Notes to Chapter 4 are on pp. 116-17.

49

aphoria between hope and persuasion that both generates and paralyzes rhetoric and thus gives the appearance of a history."[91]

The strategies of this rewriting of history involve addressing an absent other through the rhetorical gestures of doubling, loopholing, levelling, metonomy, hypallage, and parabasis, each of which will be discussed below as they are employed in the development of the idea of Unity as a social icon.

The first rhetorical gesture in which the *Task Force Report* proceeds to develop the body of Canadian Unity involves diagnostic sensitivity:

> The goal of reform . . . is not to thwart or deny these realities which are an integral part of Canadian life, but to accommodate them more adequately, to accept and channel them within Canada as a whole so that all might prosper from their presence.[92]

How is an adequate reform to be achieved? The *Report* asserts that a balance must be struck between the confederate body and its double, the conflict body. Both must be seen as equally deserving of attention; both must be given equal time. The first three chapters articulated a crisis, which at first seems too diffuse to pinpoint, but which is later "discovered" to have emerged first from Quebec. This discovery led Task Force researchers to isolate Quebec as an instigating force that has to be confronted before the entire country (bureaucratic order) will be destroyed: "We recognize that a willingness to preserve a flexible constitution depends in part on the security and confidence of the constituent units, and we will suggest a variety of ways of coping with this."[93]

Adequacy in rewriting the conflict, already identified as emerging from a Quebec-based social body, involves a flexibility that is not open-ended. "We believe that any general reform, however well intended, which fails to enhance duality or which offends the principle of regionalism is unlikely to increase harmony and unity in Canada."[94] The tropes bend in only one direction, always curling back to one solution, a particular form of Unity. The bend that can go in only one direction is a writing strategy that Bakhtin, in his study of Dostoyevsky's writing, called the "loophole."[95] Some of Dostoyevsky's characters speak in such a way that they fulfill their own wishes/fears. Each makes a hole, as it were, in her/his statements which (s)he could later move toward, having anticipated this movement in all former speech, as though expressing something of what is desired helps to bring it about. Such loopholing movement produces speech-wishes, which must be distinguished from actual changes in social reality. Change does not occur simply when one speaks of it, or because one anonymous writing wants a particular kind of change. Loopholing, as discursive desire, requires acrobatic writing, which can be found in the *Task Force Report* ("A federal system is much more supple and accommodating than most people believe"[96]). The gesture of the loophole teaches diagnostic reading skills to citizens as being important to professional patriotism. Productive change involves constitutional reform but also imaginative thinking, which is to be attended to by citizens themselves, but which is also to be based upon Task Force proposals. Hence, imaginative thinking here means federally guided diagnostic thinking, not only concerning contemporary political realities, but also about historical conditions.

The "primitive" genre of mythologizing is the type of discourse out of which the anonymous diagnosis emerges. How myth stands behind ideology was explained by the anthropologist Malinowski in his discussion of the function of myth. Malinowski began to develop new methods for studying folklore and demonstrated that studies of legend, myth, and ritual could make significant contributions to many disciplines, most notably sociology. He understood sociology primarily as the study of the ways in which groups have established courses of action in relation to myth.

> The function of myth, briefly, is to strengthen tradition and endow it with a greater value and prestige by tracing it back to a higher, better, more super-natural reality of initial events. Every historical change creates its mythology, which is, however, but indirectly related to historical fact.[97]

In the *Task Force Report*, the myth of Canada is rewritten first by tracing back, by rhetorically levelling and erasing tradition, and then replacing it with a new "higher, better" historical symbol, for example, a body of Unity unlike anything Canadians have ever before thought. Diagnosis transforms myth in the interest of the production of Unity-thought. For instance, a federal government brochure entitled "Think Canadian," written in the Department of Regional Industrial Expansion in 1985, states:

> Every Canadian can contribute to the broad economic and social gains to be achieved by considering the purchase of Canadian goods and services when price, quality and availability are competitive. "Think Canadian" is the theme of a co-operative and comprehensive domestic marketing program designed to encourage Canadians to do just that.[98]

On one level, it is the motto for a promotion of Canadian-made goods; but thinking Canadian involves more than what one might buy. To reach thought, Canadianism must be embodied in symbols as well as signs. Unity-discourse attempts to make contact with thought and participate in thought production. The *Task Force Report* assists in this process by offering rhetorical gestures with which Unity appears to desire to be thought.

The double, the body of conflict, is levelled by being converted into an instrument. Understanding the written as diagnosis stops abruptly at the end of Chapter Three, therefore writing closure in the name of equality. Empathy is no longer required, since the conflict has been contained. Chapter Four states that the sources of conflict, having received equal time and attention, must now be uprooted. The body of conflict is a phantom body, which is now to be fought with the writing of another "more compelling" vision, "the vision which supports the preservation and reorientation of this country."[99] This writing strategy makes the irony of the loophole explicit, thereby producing discursive parabasis. Parabasis is irony that herein undoes a written tradition, without producing a morphology of earlier strategies. Paul de Man has observed that irony is an undoing. In the Task Force's parabasis, history is disfigured, appearing to be more deviant than the ironic gesture that displaced it. After parabasis, confederate tradition cannot be retraced.

> Irony is no longer a trope but the undoing the deconstructive allegory of all tropological conditions, the systematic undoing, in other words, of understanding. As such, far from closing off the tropological system, irony enforces the repetition of its aberration.[100]

The irony in this chapter involves fighting an enemy-body, a stranger (called equal) by draining it, as though it were a colony in an empire. The body of conflict is moved through a draining erasure. Written in the manner of hypallage, this symbolic body becomes a source of energy for the whole. It is identified as having resourceful attributes, properties that can make it useful to a country in need of renewal, and which can become something new. The historic confederate body is articulated in relation to this as an already assimilated aspect of everyday Canadian conscious experience. The conflict body (the double) is tapped and drained for the use of the state. The third body (noun) Unity, is written as a new, major force. Hypallage has been described by Nietzsche as follows:

> The abstract nouns are properties within and outside ourselves that are being torn away from their supports and considered to be autonomous entities. . . . Such concepts, which owe their existence only to our feelings, are posited as if they were the inner essence of things; we attribute to events a cause which in truth is only an effect. The abstractions create the illusion, as if they were the entity that causes the properties, whereas they receive their objective, iconic existence only from us as a consequence of these very properties.[101]

Hypallage is a defensive intrusion on and by language. It is an intrusion on the local and particular consciousness of ongoing reality. It can act as a syphon, attempting to drain off notions of difference and history, and working to replace these with Unity-discourse. This is very similar to the operation which Dorothy Smith would describe as ideological writing practice within documentary reality. In her terms, such drainage is a way of disorganizing thought around particular concerns such that other ways of thinking can be introduced. For example, the *Report* constantly intrudes, offering social objectives which are to be considered significant by patriots.

Such objectives need to be reflected upon before Canadians should embark on private initiatives. Only certain types of initiatives, however, will be considered useful, that is, patriotic.[102] The former confederate body must be treated with "sensitivity" and the new social force developed out of understanding. The Task Force develops its third figure, Unity, into a protagonist, as an objective mediator. "The third element is non-partisan either if he [sic] stands above the contrasting interests and opinions and is actually not concerned with them, or if he is equally concerned with both."[103]

A Contextural Turn on "Respecting Diversity"

The regional body, the body of conflict, is the body of the ear; the body of the eye cannot read ethnic speech, since it is not written anonymously, but can be heard only through a listener's understanding of the native tongue. Derrida traces one path of the native tongue when appropriated by the state.

> Dream this umbilicus: it has you by the ear. It is an ear, however, that dictates to you the very thing that passes through your ear and travels the length of the cord all the way down to your stenography. This writing links you, like a leash in the form of an umbilical cord, to the paternal belly of the state.[104]

Here, Derrida describes a social condition in which hearing can be restrained, as though the head and mind could be held on a leash. The leash is what I have been calling anonymous writing, which privileges imitative reading and writing. Derrida's description also alludes to a half-flesh, half-metal human condition in his usage of the image of a cord which becomes part of the writer, as does "stenography." The collective repetition of bureaucratic reading and writing procedures can be recognized as robot-like activities. This reading of Derrida is evoked by the foreboding tenor of the passage. He invites one to dream of the cord. But this dream is no fantasy; it is, rather, a nightmarish reality. Derrida sees citizens as children, unable to detach themselves from the enormous, mechanical, "paternal belly of the state." The cord is connected, but, as Derrida also states, readers have ears that can be used.

In the introductory section of Chapter Five of the *Report*, in which the conflict body is presented as a potential "resource," duality and ethnic regionalism are downplayed. The chapter explains that Unity will not be limiting or stifling, and cautiously declares, with a seeming flexibility, that the agenda includes "Respecting Diversity." The writing instead privileges the notion of a "new social balance produced by the impersonal forces of modernization."[105] Consider the statement, "Modernization has brought strong pressure for linguistic assimilation to English;"[106] the parabasic turn is intended to defer problems related to the volatile dual language debate. "We" have tried our best to entice provincial governments into placing English and French "on an equal footing" by making the statutory changes that these governments have been reluctant to make (without describing the reasons they give for their reluctance). "We" passed the *Official Languages Act* in 1969, and the effects of these actions are described as follows:

> The federal government's support for bilingualism, even as it has evolved over the last thirteen years, has resulted in much greater access by the Canadian public in their preferred official language to the services provided by federal institutions. . . . Of equal importance is that the proportion of francophones working in the federal administration is now approximately equal to their proportion in the population for the first time in this century, for by 1977, 27.6 per cent of federal civil servants had French as their mother tongue.[107]

Therefore, equality in language policy teaches the patriot to measure success bureaucratically. The number of francophones working as civil servants marks the degree of success achieved in attempts to inscribe the unruly mother, the culture of the spoken tongue, *la langue*.

"It is vital that the language policy of the central government command broad popular support."[108] It is vital because this support will serve to sustain the federal body as the new body of Unity. "We" are willing to find ways to weigh and

measure oral culture. "We" will continue to try to persuade
provincial governments to see the value in this effort. They
must come to understand how vital the draining of the body
of conflict is to Canada's future, even if it means allowing
special privileges for "frenchness."[109] It does not really seem
to matter to Task Force writers what rights Quebec is given
as long as she remains in Canada. In fact, it is the legal right
of specialness given in writing that returns Quebec to Canada. As Auguste Comte observed concerning the matter of
rights:

> The word Right should be excluded from political lan-
> guage.... Every one has duties, duties towards all; but
> rights in the ordinary sense can be claimed by none. What-
> ever security the individual may require is found in the gen-
> eral acknowledgement of reciprocal obligations; and this
> gives a moral equivalent for rights as hitherto claimed, with-
> out the serious political dangers which they involved.[110]

Special consideration for "frenchness" can only be given
by the Task Force as a promise devised under the emblem of
Canada, in return for which is expected another promise,
that of the patriotic oath. Quebec is not the only form associated with the figure of the conflict-body; the Task Force
writes Quebec as the catalyst for crisis, yet repercussions, as
they exist in other places, must also be dealt with. In fact,
the Task Force uses cultural diversity as a tactic for promot-
ing a particular notion of "rights" across the board.

"Today those of non-British or non-French origin represent more than a quarter of our population."[111] This statistic
is presented as a way of decentring the local concerns of particular ethnic or native groups. No community has the
"right" to present their concerns as unique; since the whole
of Canada is made up of such unique groups, local interests
must be re-articulated. The general issue is one of pluralism,
not regionalism, and this pluralism is best served, with
rights most adequately maintained, by federal and provincial
jurisdictions.

> The regional or provincial framework is the one in which
> the various ethnic communities have been able to organize
> and express themselves most effectively and in which plu-
> ralism has become a living social reality. It is for this rea-

son that we believe Canadian pluralism should be closely linked, in thought and in action, to Canadian regionalism.[112]

The link between regionalism and provincialism is forged through pluralism. But the term pluralism on its own means nothing, being too abstract, too obscure. So the *Report* adds culture to pluralism as an adjective with abundant associations: "Cultural pluralism has achieved its greatest importance at the provincial level and it is there that it should be most fully reflected and nurtured."[113] Provinces have been plural and the state has been dual. In unity-thought, however, to think in terms of the double as traditional is to produce analysis; to orient towards achieving unity is to produce a patriotic diagnosis. Gradually, the plural nature of local communities comes to be renamed and reorganized; the plural undergoes a process of transformation whereby it becomes the "regional." Regional practices, then, come to be defined as cultural artifacts that are co-ordinated at the provincial level; however, the definitions that the provinces will use to determine "culture" originate with the federal government. Provincial culture is what stimulates a taste for a unified Canadian style. Therefore culture will also be redefined in this rewriting of Canada's body. Culture will be what is considered resourceful in pluralism, that which can be defined as a regional resource.

George Melnyk has pointed out that regional culture loses its originality when it becomes absorbed by a centralized cultural consciousness. A unique, local artifact, for instance, can be made the solution, the transitory centrepiece in the search for Canadian identity. When this occurs, a particular community loses its identity. "The culture that occasionally arises from the hinterland to be absorbed by metropolitan culture stops being for itself and becomes for the other."[114] When local culture has already been exploited, regional or "hinterland" culture will be named as such, and will take on a role which would be in contrast with, or even oppose, other forms of cultural production. Regionalism can thus be seen as a federally developed social, discursive icon. Inuit art is one example of a local indigenous practice which has become a thriving Canadian industry.

Native Peoples

Native peoples are called "First Canadians" in the *Task Force Report*. They are seen as one people, not many, and include Inuit people.

> The exclusive federal authority over all matters that touch
> "Indianess," as the present chief justice of Canada has put
> it, is unique in giving to the Parliament of Canada legisla-
> tive jurisdiction in relation to a specified group of people.
> For administrative and policy purposes, just who is and
> who is not "Indian" is set out in the *Indian Act*.[115]

It is very important for administrators to be able to clearly define who is and who is not Indian for three reasons. For one, members of Indian and Inuit tribes do not have to pay taxes. For another, most groups have been relegated to reserves, parcels of land upon which they are "allowed" to live by the federal government. Only true natives are allowed to live for "free" with special Indian "rights" in these areas. Thirdly, their cultural resources are of a different order from those identifiable as the "regional" cultures of pluralism.

The *Report* presents four options (in a loophole) which address the issue of how to bring the native people into the future Canada. The first option is entitled "Phasing out special status," which would involve terminating the assistance programs to native people, and settling all "sound" land claims. Titles would be transferred to natives, who would then be left to fend for themselves within Canadian society at large. The *Report* suggests that native people themselves object to this idea very strongly, and it interprets their wish as being to have both special status and land claims. The second option is called a "modified federal role." Designed to accommodate both special status and land claims, this policy concept would also include giving First Canadians a choice: to either stay on the reserve or to "move into the mainstream of Canadian society." They would be assisted in making and implementing their choices (designed as choices by federal policy-makers) by one centrally co-ordinated government department.[116]

The third option is described as "Native sovereignty." This is articulated as a radical desire on the part of some natives to attempt to return to the peace and autonomy that they think their ancestors may have experienced prior to the great white invasion of North America. First Canadians favouring this option would set up "autonomous institutions within the Canadian federal system." Although still in some sense citizens, natives would then "be subject to laws and regulations of their own making, and in some versions [of the wish], would not be subject to central, provincial and municipal laws and regulations on their land."[117] The final option, "Citizens plus," is the option preferred by the Task Force. This "choice" combines some elements of the other options; the "plus" refers to Canada's never-ending obligation, a debt to be repaid to the native "people." This debt would inform the spirit in which natives would continue to receive special rights from the federal government.

> Thus, while specific programs of assistance to native people may change with changing circumstances, the spirit of Canada's special commitment would not. Their well-being would form a mixed priority of the highest importance to Canadians now and in the future.[118]

The rights to be changed, which would make native citizens "plus," are articulated by way of five recommendations.

1. Amendments to Sections 11 and 12 of the *Indian Act* would ensure that native women gain status "equal" to that of Indian men.
2. Native languages and cultures should be better protected and more widely promoted. Canadian native peoples should have more opportunities to meet with the native people of other countries. This is suggested so that "Canada can show leadership in a field of international affairs at once new and of historic significance."[119]
3. The native constitutional position must be reconsidered interactively with native representatives.
4. The federal and provincial governments would determine the agencies or persons responsible for various native services.
5. Funding would be given to First Canadians so that they can research and write their own native histories. They

would also be invited to sit on boards and task forces when such committees are reviewing topics pertinent to the first people.

This last recommendation is particularly intriguing because it seems to combine two unrelated topics — native historical research, and native corporate/bureaucratic input. The *Report* seems to be saying that the Indians or Inuit who have developed historical expertise can act as experts in both the public and private sectors. Another reading is related by the sentence that concludes this section of the *Report*.

> Governments generally and major private sector corporations should make greater efforts to see that native people are adequately represented on boards and commissions, task forces and study groups which are active in fields of special relevance to the First Canadians.[120]

What fields are to be considered not of "special relevance" to First Canadians? Why should they be invited to sit on some boards and not on others? And why should they be given funds to research only their own histories? Because they are being told to join in, to become more indigenous — to become First Canadians. Nevertheless, they can be Canadians only to a certain degree. The "plus" in their citizenship will only heighten the awareness of their stigma; it is a sign which points to "they" as those who must be kept on the margins. The native peoples remember other lands with other traditions, before there was any Canada and before there were any Canadians. They will never participate fully in "our" history; therefore, they cannot be asked to participate in the remembrance of historical rewritings.

The First Canadians are being told to focus on themselves, to keep to their own histories and to their own special interests. They will not be invited to sit on any and every commission because they can never become patriots. The government owes them because of what they cannot forget; thus they will never be considered resourceful. Instead, they are always only a handicap in and to the social body. The loophole is the extension of their marginality. In the past, their special status, although problematic, recognized natives as different, but now, the native stigma is named with the aid of a chiasmus: those who cannot be Canadians first shall be called First Canadians. Their options are erased in a writing that denies the realities of their difference. This is a prime example of Smith's understanding of documents in negotiating reality. Those who know how such documents attempt to define reality can become empowered if they articulate themselves into the process. Those who cannot do this will be summarily written out.

Cultural Policy

Culture, finally, takes on two meanings.

> Culture may refer to what many would call the "high culture," on display in the theatres, museums, concert halls and art galleries. However, in its broadest meaning, culture includes the complete fabric, values and life of a community. If this is what is meant by culture, it seems clear that the provinces have, and ought to have, a larger role to play in the formation of cultural policy.[121]

"High" culture is defined as "the kind of cultural policies which would now be appropriate for the central government."[122] The policies would include the creation of more prizes and competitions for talented young artists, the promotion of Canadian books, paintings, and films, and the sending of students to other regions for immersion and exchange programs. The overall impact of federal cultural policy then becomes an attempt to educate local individuals into understanding which Canadian artistic products are to be considered "good" and "tasteful" works. First Canadians will gain federal approval for fitting native arts and culture.

Popular culture is to be handled through councils of the provincial governments. To receive funding the groups would have to be determined by their respective provinces to be producing local forms of art that "promote the ideal of direct public participation in regional and cultural development."[123] Hence, local artists who believe in the regional ideals of their province would be given support for their projects. Furthermore, the local communities that promote appropriate ideals of Canadianism would be contributing to culture through "non-cultural" programs in a manner considered by the

Report as vital "for the development of young citizens of the federation of the whole."[124] "High" culture must compete within international circles; "low" culture need only gain provincial support, the provinces being critical agents for the federal government. The promotion of an appropriate understanding of Unity is defined as the most important cultural activity. This point is made emphatically with reference to cultural production in Quebec.

> Thus the provinces, and in particular Quebec, have an essential responsibility for culture in its most basic sense. The central government, while not ignoring its appropriate role, must be prepared to recognize this fact and should orient its own future activity to cultural endeavors and institutions which affect the federation as a whole.[125]

Reading the "Unity and Health of the Economy"

> Intergovernmental conflicts over taxation, marketing boards and provincial purchasing policies were raised as major subjects of concern.
> We take these views as additional evidence to support our conviction that Canada's crisis has economic, social, political and psychological dimensions — all intimately related.[126]

Chapter Six is associated with health — that of a robust body which can fight off the national identity crisis/illness and still encompass "regional" interests. It begins by abstracting from the statements of citizens who brought their concerns about the state of the Canadian economy before the Task Force. The opinions offered by citizens are described as if they were facts in two ways. First, the citizens' concerns are collected into sentences that identify "major areas of concern." This developed from the method of co-ordinating individual accounts into edited versions (presented throughout Volume Three of the *Report* as "The Views of the Public") that were then edited again into generalized statements. Beng-Huat Chua, in his analysis of the *B & B Commission* has called this editing process a "reorganization of the supportive opinions to formulate the problem."[127] Second, private, critical concerns are presented as specific kinds of limited knowledge, which are forms of "analysis" that are not informed by the broader perspective developed by the federal government, and articulated in a diagnosis that can make links. Patriots must be able to connect what is healthy (in the Task Force's efforts to create a new sense of unity) with what is traditional and familiar. The body of Unity is elaborated here by way of an economic description, in an attempt to make it familiar: "The link between the health of the economy and efforts to sustain unity is a theme that recurs in Canada's history."[128]

The effort to integrate citizens' concerns, viewed as under-informed facts, with well-informed federal facts, is a rhetorical device called suturing. To suture is to take two apparently disconnected concepts and link them together. It works best when employed in the interest of discovery. Suturing becomes arbitrary and stilted when the investigator knows in advance what (s)he wishes the suture to produce. This device was also used to make natives into First Canadians. In Chapter Five the suturing of the "they" and the "not-quite-us" produced the term "the people," as one feature of diagnosis. Every time diagnosis has come into play, the *Report* elaborates a viewpoint on the body of conflict, and Chapter Six is consistent in this regard.

> In traditionally strong export markets for forestry products, minerals and other raw materials, Canada faces severe competition, primarily from the emerging states of the Third World.
>
> More important, the challenge of restructuring and managing Canada's economy has to be met while recognizing the realities of modern Quebec and the aspirations of Canada's regional communities.[129]

The advantages of economic association for regions within the Canadian whole and as one federation are written such that they include the ability to specialize in the forms of production in which specific regions have a particular advantage, as well as having the ability to benefit from federal programs concerned with "economic adjustment." To require adjustment implies that there has been a dislocation. Technology is identified as a major cause of provincial malaise. Economic adjustment involves helping provinces cope fiscally with technological transition. The federal government can perform "interregional transfers of public funds" to sustain provinces during difficult periods of economic adjustment.[130] Managing Canada's economy means managing the economy of all provinces and territories. Quebec must be appeased in a way that will allow its resources to compete and to represent Canada in the international marketplace, and such that Quebec's revenues will be available for transfer when deemed necessary. Regional economies are said to gain much in the way of international trade, and are given up-to-the-minute information on areas of product specialization that they should focus on. Allocation of various aspects of production is discussed under the topic of competition, which, when it occurs between sectors of the economy, is taken to be a good thing, while competition between provinces is not. Regional economies must be co-ordinated in such a way that competing interests (in terms of provincial revenue) work to produce an overall surplus of resources.

> In a nutshell, integration creates a surplus, because the whole is greater than its parts. And the surplus, using the central government as an instrument, can be redistributed so that the strong parts help the weak to benefit the whole.[131]

Here, readers are given a first hint of one of the characteristics of the body of Unity that will emerge from the integration of the confederate and the conflict bodies. Surplus is a descriptive noun employed to outline Unity's body. The surplus aspect of the body is important because it is supposedly a feature which sustains all parts of the whole.

Quebec is described as being "swollen by its own particular problem."[132] As such, the body of conflict has a pregnant (blossoming) belly; however, it is misdiagnosed by federal practitioners as being distended from (patriotic) malnutrition, and in need of nourishment from the whole. In other words, it is written as having a starving belly that is unaware of impending starvation, an anorexic aspect of the Canadian social framework. Unaware that it needs national nourishment, the conflict-body takes delight in the swelling of its belly, which is read as a warning sign by *Report* researchers; if Quebec stays isolated within its own particular limited viewpoint, a viewpoint written as being "confused," then its "swelling" could prove fatal. "What péquistes have in mind, as far as anyone can tell, is some kind of one-to-one association between Quebec and the rest of Canada."[133] This is the way Quebec's "confusion" has been articulated in the *Report*. The péquiste dream is later written as something that must be fought by a dream that is less confused, that is, the federal, comprehensive, all-encompassing dream of Canadian Unity.

Bryan Turner, in his book *The Body & Society* describes the social bind of anorexia as follows: "Anorexia is the product of contradictory social pressures on women of affluent families and an anxiety directed at the surface of the body in a system organized around narcissistic consumption"[134] and "By denying her sexuality as a personal choice, the anorexic accepts, or at least conforms to, an ethic of consumer sexuality."[135]

The body of conflict looks anorexic to the Task Force diagnosticians because of a seemingly fantastic self-conception produced within the body of conflict. The notion that a separate swelling could be anything other than disastrous for Canada is interpreted as narcissistic by unity-thought and thus as subversive, even to its own "health," which is assumed to be dependent upon one unified state. The *Report* produces a logic that invites the supposedly starving body of conflict to be federally sustained so that it can become "well" and then it will be able to help "enlarge the surplus." In order to become more resourceful, more useful to the body of Unity, Quebec in particular must acknowledge the social organism of surplus. Canada can only function properly if there is one belly, one digestive tract (and one womb). The assumption is that two social organisms split asunder the economic/nutritional system. The misdiagnosed anorexic body, in refusing to be a parasite, instead becomes a host.[136] To this end, the *Report* urges the double (including its regional aspects) to

1. abandon preferential purchasing policies,
2. participate in the development of national standards in the professions and trades,

3. encourage, by way of provincial legislation, the free movement of capital in land deals and corporate mergers,
4. co-ordinate taxation policies with the other provinces "in order to prevent fiscal competition that would seriously distort the preferences of businesses and individuals with respect to location,"[137] and finally to
5. consent to the federal government's control over monetary policy for the purposes of stabilization: "the term stabilization refers to the conscious variation of government taxation, expenditure, and borrowing which counteract business cycles and maintain the pace of activity close to the potential of the economy."[138]

Two areas over which the federal government would like to have control are energy and other non-renewable resources, and industrial strategy, which is regarded as "the main weapon of economic adjustment."[139]

These recommendations are said to be mutually beneficial to both the provinces and the nation. Focussing specifically on Quebec's "swelling," the *Report* explains that, based on trade studies, "Quebec's economy is highly dependent upon the Canadian common market."[140] The standard of living of the average francophone living in Quebec, the *Report* cites, is below that of individuals in other provinces because of the "deterioration in the competitive position of weak manufacturing industries, the vulnerability of resource-based industries to changing international conditions, an inadequate rate of economic development, and an insufficiently mobile labour force."[141] This list of problem areas within Quebec's economy will best be resolved, the *Report* insists, if Quebec contributes to the surplus, which will benefit all as long as there is economic union.

Quebec is represented as being vulnerable to the PQ's desire to separate from Canada, and this is interpreted as a morbid desire. In response, the *Report* states that Ottawa will not threaten or beg Quebec into staying within the original confederate body. Such tactics, however, do not work when treating bodies diagnosed as anorexic. They must be inspired to appropriate usage of the province's mouth. Or, more precisely, Quebec is to be the mouth of Canada's body.

What is needed instead is that Quebecers be shown that they can have a more promising future within confederation than outside of it. To this effect, we are convinced that the Canadian federation can be restructured and can achieve a better overall balance that would both suit and support a distinctive character for Quebec.[142]

The *Report* intends to present to Quebec a "restructured," future-oriented federal body, with whom she must learn to speak Canada's third language. As well as the two official languages, the anonymous symbolizations represented in this *Report*, and in others to come, constitute what can be called a diagnostic grammar of constitutional-ese.

Proposal for "A Restructured Federalism"

A strong, but compassionate organism, promoted as "A Restructured Federalism," is described in Chapter Seven, which is the longest and most technical chapter of the *Report*. Yet if the reader were only interested in the technicalities associated with constitutional reform, (s)he need only flip to Chapter Nine, which is a point-form summary of the technical recommendations made throughout the entire *Report*. Chapter Seven, however, discloses a great deal about the nature of the body of Unity. First, Unity will emerge from a "creative" effort within bureaucratic structures as these are already organized.

The deep-rooted crisis before Canada calls for a more systematic approach than a negotiated consensus between central and provincial governments on a number of discrete topics will provide. To achieve such a systematic resolution will require our political leaders at both levels of government to rise above traditional jealousies and to achieve a spirit of creativeness and innovation, such as that which existed in the 1860s when out of political crisis and deadlock Confederation was conceived.[143]

This implies that the practices of governing can be a form of cultural production. The body of Unity is meant to be an inspired creation of two levels of government, the federal government's contribution being "to sustain, encourage and symbolize . . . to ensure . . . to have an overriding responsibility . . . to control . . . to oversee . . . to stimulate." The provincial governments in these instances are assigned fewer infinitive verbs ("to tax . . . to establish . . . to sign"). However, the *Report* states that they should also have

> exclusive (or occasionally concurrent) jurisdiction over matters pertaining to culture, education, health, social services, marriage and divorce, immigration, manpower and training, the administration of justice, natural resources including fisheries, regional economic development, trade within the province, consumer and corporate affairs, urban affairs, housing and land use, and environment.[144]

Through the right kind of federal and provincial collaboration, a new constitution will be written and implemented. This artifact is intended "to meet the aspirations and future needs of all the people of Canada."[145] The new constitution will be the skeleton of the body of Unity, whose inscribed body's (paternal) belly will need nourishment (through the umbilicus of oath) from all of the provinces in order to reach a level of surplus. Although handicapped in the pursuit of absolute patriotic obedience by native and ethnic interests ("the Canadian federation, like others, from the beginning has never been, nor can it be, totally symmetrical"[146]) there can nevertheless be a form of constitutionally defined symmetry at the federal level. "[T]he central government may in certain instances be given specific powers to override otherwise normally exclusive provincial powers, for example in emergencies."[147] Furthermore, "there may be wider potential for uniform central laws to be combined with flexible provincial enforcement."[148]

Chua has noted that the state continually attempts to persuade citizens, first, that the economy is in need of being saved, and, second, that the government is always hard at work saving it "in the best interests of every member whenever possible, even when these best interests may often result in personal hardships for some segment of the society."[149] This "best interest" is the *Report*'s "we." The work of saving is in one sense the work of continually revising and redefining "us" over against "them."

The *Report* shows that it is constrained by the very double it has written. Canada, as federally organized, is unrecognizable without the body of conflict. She must be persuaded to contribute to unity, no matter what forms of special status will be required to bring this about, since her separation "would lead to the rupture of Canada."[150] But the other provinces may become resentful if Quebec is seen to be privileged. Therefore,

> the more preferable approach is to allot to all provinces powers in the areas needed by Quebec to maintain its distinctive culture and heritage, but to do so in a manner which would enable the other provinces, if they so wished, not to exercise these responsibilities and leave them instead to Ottawa.[151]

A process of allotment is interdependent with the monitoring of how responsibilities are being exercised, but no mention is made of process and allotment as issues of concern in the *Report*. Processes are downplayed in favour of "subjects," in the sense of subject matter: "The expanded activity of both levels of government has given to almost every subject both a federal and provincial aspect."[152] Nowhere is mention made of human subjects or subjectivity, and yet, all citizens are subject to constitutional and other legal codes. The organization of subject matters with "both federal and provincial aspects" has previously been handled, the *Report* explains, by what have been called executive groups:

> The need for institutions to reconcile and harmonize the objectives of both orders of government is attested to by the spontaneous growth in recent years of a wide network of intergovernmental meetings and conference [*sic*], at both the ministerial and official levels. This network of conferences has come to be known as "executive federalism" because of the way it responds to the new reality of interdependence through direct negotiations between the executives of both orders of government.[153]

The existence of such executives marks the degree of corporate co-ordination present in government procedure. The *Report* sees a tendency towards a confusion between public and private institutional interests in this arrangement, and therefore wishes to incorporate negotiators into the federal government structure. "In order to do this the present Senate would be replaced by a second chamber of the Canadian Parliament in the form of a council of representatives of the provincial governments."[154] This second chamber, called the Council of the Federation, would be composed of a delegation from each province and territory, headed by ministers. These representatives would receive and negotiate instructions from their respective provincial governments. Such a council would also be created to offset tensions that emerge when one level of government has acted on occasion without consulting the other. The *Report* writers wish to make federal and provincial governments subject to each other, equally balanced on the pen of the mediating Council. The Council of the Federation would be a diagnostic tribunal, watchful for any re-emergence of the body of conflict's "illness." It would also operate under new definitions of (instructions for the development of) consensus.

The writing of the body of Unity has redefined culture. What is culturally "best" is that which contains the "right" type of national sentiment. Canadian federalist culture can forget and can therefore always reproduce patriotism. Patriots are those who allow themselves to be rewritten, that is, who allow their statements to be edited and developed into Task Force facts. Patriots consent to being reshaped in light of a new writing of Canadian history, and in so doing, subjectivity becomes subject matter. Each attentive citizen is a minor character in the allegory of the three bodies. Some emerge as protagonists, on the side of the body of Unity, while those who do "analysis" are aligned with the "ill" and angry body of conflict.

Allegory is an ideological feature of the *Task Force Report*. When one examines ideology by way of genre analysis, the three bodies form an emblem. To emblematize is to allegorize. Dualism refers to the arcane confederal society, the social body which was sustained by rough and ready citizens. Regional character is another description attributed to the present body of conflict, the remote, oral, analytic body of the "they." Unity is the diagnostic body of the future. The model for sharing patriots, the conflict body, will become surplus, that is, "healthy"—it will lose its distention—once the body of conflict is convinced to share and become part of the "we."

The next chapter will explore this concept as a perversion of a mythology that inscribes Canada in an anonymous history of a future Unity, and rewrites the so-called chaotic present of many interest groups into a more manageable Canadian past that remembers Quebec as the source of agitation concerning duality, ethnic rights and autonomy. This is a shift in the symbolic code from myth to allegory, for, "efforts have been made to create or preserve physical manifestations of Canada and its heritage, a task undertaken by both federal and provincial authorities."[155]

On the literal level, "physical manifestations" refers to historic preservation and conservation. But this explanation only (barely) explains the use of the verb "preserve." How does Canada, as "both federal and provincial authorities" seek to create a heritage? My answer to this is: by constructing symbolic protagonists, and introducing ways of rethinking about why and how to be Canadian. The protagonist who emerges from the *Task Force Report* is the body of Unity. This characterization is developed using allegorical narrative strategies. Allegory is a highly moralistic genre. It is the moral attitude of Unity as protagonist that gives the *Report* descriptive power.

5 Mytho-history to Allegory: Tomorrow's Unity as Patriot's Progress

From Community to Leviathan

In his book *Five Bodies*, John O'Neill describes the development of the concept of the social body in older societies. He laments that individuals have lost the connection between their bodies and society, and he believes that a disconnection occurred with the intrusion of a medicalized body, which is interdependent with a consumer body. Both are ways of thinking about the body as something that can be manipulated with instruments made available in the marketplace, e.g., drugs, plastic surgery, makeup. He asserts that the connection remains between the body and the social, even though some social actors may not be aware of this. His position rests on the following three assumptions: (1) "the rational construction of the cosmos is possible only on the ground of that first poetic logic whereby people thought the world with their bodies";[156] (2) "just as we think society with our bodies so, too, [do] we think our bodies with society";[157] and (3) "the body politic is the fundamental structure of our political life."[158]

The modern concept of the social body is a powerful bureaucratic narrative strategy. Social bodies in small, tribal societies have been highly particularized conceptions of the world, quite different from the anatomical conceptions of feudal and modern states. O'Neill does not distinguish between tribal anthropomorphizing and Western philosophical body

Notes to Chapter 5 are on pp. 117-18.

construction other than to identify one as primary and the other as inevitable. It can be argued that the tribal body was immediate, local, oral, and irreducibly subjective, while the modern societal body is distant, documentary, economic (as an apparatus of Capital), and wholly other in the interest, first and foremost, of social order. Hobbes's "Common-Wealth" and Comte's "Humanity," among other macrosocial images, moved Bryan Turner to write that "the teleological purposiveness of the body was employed to legitimate political and social divisions in society."[159]

How these divisions became established can be explained in many ways. My interest is in the reproduction of community mores, which were transmitted in stories of good and evil, adventure, battle, and love, in the form of oral folktales. Whatever threads of mytho-history that remain now comprise the body of local practice — those aspects of collective memory that remember the community as family, as a "thinking body."[160] Assuming that there are remaining threads, I posit that there are at least two textural surfaces in/on the written. In the case of the *Task Force Report*, one surface is the anonymous rewriting of Canadian history. Another texture that I have discovered in this written version of the state is a battle narrative framed as an allegory, and rooted in mythology. The texture of the polis-as-written is a loose weave of overlapping histories and story-telling traditions.

Within "primitive" cosmologies, human existence was a minute segment of a much larger reality; realms of gods and ancestors invisible to the organic eye, but quite clear to the mind's eye, surrounded the world of physical beings. Nature and ancestor spirits visited the earthly realm, usually appearing in day and night dreams. Shamans became the mediators who travelled to netherworlds and brought back cures and advice. Medieval societies were among those in which the invisible world came to earth in the form of aristocrats and administrators as mediators for ancestor spirits. As representatives of gods, the kings, lords, and priests became all-powerful. Their minstrel songs and allegorical morality plays were designed, not for the emancipation of common people, but for the reproduction of hierarchical systems. For example, the character "Covetousness" advises

Piers Plowman: "Take thy money to the Bishop / bid him use it for thy soul; / He shall answer for thee / at the High Judgement Day, / For thee — and many more."[161]

The myth-allegory difference can be traced to changes in society that were brought about by the organization and maintenance of feudal states. Machiavelli suggested to his readers that orderly states were those which appropriated and manipulated local, traditional beliefs for their own systematic purposes. Such states

> are sustained by ancient religious customs, which are so powerful and of such quality, that they keep their princes in power in whatever manner they proceed and live. These princes alone have states without defending them, have subjects without governing them, and their states, not being defended, are not taken from them; their subjects not being governed do not resent it, and neither think nor are capable of alienating themselves.[162]

The appropriation of ancestral beliefs for administrative ends occurred within many areas of oral cultures that were in transition, most notably in courtly plays, stories, and songs.[163] The transition can be thought of as a site of collision among locally articulated cosmologies; when smaller isolated communities were arbitrarily fused into larger "bodies," mores and rites from various constituencies came into conflict. To quote again from *Piers Plowman*: "No man can serve two masters."[164] Conflicts were usually resolved by judges/priests, who through their interpretations of disputes developed laws which came to act as the written symbols of an over-riding cosmology, that of the written rule of the state. Edmund Leach has speculated that myth was the central text used to teach tribe members who desired access to the power of divine signs. Those who most clearly understood the signs became, at least in part, divine themselves. "In mythology," states Leach, "the mediating bridge can be occupied by incarnate deities, who manage, by an elision of metaphor and metonymy, to be both human beings and gods at the same time."[165]

In tribal societies, travelling to the worlds of the divine and speaking to spirits gave one power and the authority to advise members, while in medieval societies, having state power made one divine. Myth became a participant in the

shift from the local to the state body, and its characterization
assisted in the appropriation and alienation of community
members. Myth's first function was to articulate, in a creative
and magical way, the relations and connections that were
already vital and apparent to members, but were unspoken.
Unspoken social factors ranging from birthright to ownership
were dramatized for the powerful in the middle ages. What
one king owned another might conquer if undefended. In *Le
Charroi de Nimes* for example, William the Conqueror's conquest of the city of Orange adds insult to injury when he steals
the ruler's wife, Orable, and takes her for his own. Jacques Le
Goff describes how "the chanson ends with the baptism of
Orable, who becomes the Christian woman Guibourc and mar-
ries William, a logical consequence of the capture of a city
which is also the capture of a woman."[166] Important to the
relation between religion and conquest is that Orable, symbolic of the city itself, was not only captured but was also converted. In allowing herself to be displaced, she represents how
cities could endure a change of rulers and thus survive. In this
allegory's message, a change of religion need not unduly harm
the life of a beautiful city. In *Le Charroi de Nimes*, Orable
changes rulers, husbands and religions; both she and her city
remain relatively intact. Religious change, then, was to be
understood first and foremost as administrative revision.

Every Reader's Unity

Report writing, it could be argued, is far too simple and
straightforward a form to have any connection to literary
genres. Yet because the *Task Force Report* foreshadows law in
the form of a new constitution, its writers produced a moral
vision to accompany the new policies for new patriots; "allegory
returns to ever simpler patterns of action. The mode is radically reductive."[167] Following Fletcher, the Task Force needed
an anthropomorphic emblem, one with utopian dimensions,
and one which could find a "fit" in the imagination of the reading citizen. The process of seeking a match involves more than
agreement with the economic and legal intentions set forth in
the *Task Force Report*. It involves effecting a link to significant
symbols; this means that there must be a desire to obtain con-

sensus on the cognitive level, within the associative and projective processes of reader-citizens. This level of "fit" is what Task Force writers hoped that citizens would strive for in their reading in order to be transformed into patriots.

Allegory is a highly restrictive literary form. It is complex when reading but very linear to write. By this I mean, it follows a recipe. Anyone can produce an allegory by following the steps. It may not be a masterwork, but playing with exaggerated, distant, anthropomorphized virtues and vices will inevitably lead even the poorest of writers towards a moral. Such a formula is required when many persons work to produce one set of documents. Further, allegory's penchant for extremes inevitably produces another time and place; the writing of a separate realm, emerging from a distinct set of expectations, enables the *Report* to look objective.

> Allegory perhaps has a "reality" of its own, but it is certainly not of the sort that operates in our perceptions of the physical world. It has an idealizing consistency of thematic content, because, in spite of the visual absurdity of much allegorical imagery, the relations between ideas are under strong logical control.[168]

Allegory presents a systematized, metaphoric cosmology designed to fascinate. The *Task Force Report* writers attempted to write in an inspiring manner, to elicit intense feeling — a patriotic fervour. This fervour is supposed to rouse citizens from apathy and to develop in them a strong desire for participation. Everyone's energy is needed to help bring about Unity. The *Report*'s prescription for apathy (as analysis) is to focus passionately on reading Canada as the body of Unity as it is produced in writing. There are many written precedents for such fervour. The character of the Doctor concludes the morality play *Everyman* as follows:

> Ye hearers, take it of worth, old and young, / And forsake pride, for he deceiveth you in the end, / And remember Beauty, Five-wits, Strength, and Discretion, / They all at the last do Everyman forsake, / Save his Good-Deeds, there doth he take.[169]

The attributes which Everyman finally realizes to be of greatest value are his accumulated good deeds. Good-Deeds is an allegorical figure who has come to life, as a friend, to aid Everyman in his final hour. Those who rally round in times of crisis, therefore, constitute faithful friends. Only those who know how to perform certain kinds of deeds, called good, can be of assistance in a time of dire need. The *Task Force Report* could have been alternately named Good-Deeds.

History, economics, and cultural production pervade both surfaces of the *Report*. The textural surface of the research is written as the discovery of social facts which can help or hinder Canadian Unity. The texture of allegory is written as moral logic, as a series of propositions which redefine good and evil; the propositions are written, and taken-for-granted assumptions about the "shape" of Canadian consciousness. This shape must have the potential to draw out a reader's expectations, such that the text and the reader together weave an image which will bring about a textural consensus. Agreement must first occur between a text and one reader. But the expectation of consensus requires agreement between the text and every single reader.

The creation of Unity "among Canadians" means that the Unity-body can emerge only out of consensus, the agreement to share in a common vision of Canada's future. Chapter Eight of the *Report* suggests that a legal document, even a new constitution, is not a sufficiently vital image to arouse Canadians to patriotism. "[I]t will be easier to change the constitution than it will be to create unity among Canadians."[170] Bakhtin formulated a writing strategy which he called re-accentuation, the taking of an image that has had power for readers and articulating it in another/new context.

Rabelais's Gargantua, for instance, was the prototype for Swift's Gulliver. Piers Plowman and Everyman were prototypes for Bunyan's allegorical figure of the Christian. Threads from all of these inform the *Task Force Report*'s protagonistic body of Unity. The unified and "vital" body of Canada is what citizens are supposed to focus on, and the reader's attention is turned to the written bodies and away from its researchers/writers. Reader-citizens are invited to pledge allegiance to an allegorical body, a protagonist-in-potential which can only come to "exist" once it is believed collectively.

In a democratic age it is probably necessary, in order to establish the unity of a country, to secure some measure of accord among its citizens. The citizens, as well as their political leaders, must take responsibility for the welfare of their country and the vitality of their collective life.[171]

The Climax of Canada's Rewriting

"Let us, in concluding, return to the beginning." Thus, the *Report*'s beginning is best presented at its end, and Chapter Eight is presented as a conclusion that articulates a new beginning, a healthy future Canada.

We are not sure that our vision of Canada will meet the approval of all Canadians, but we have become convinced, over the months we have met as a task force, that our three principles of duality, regionalism and the sharing of benefits and power form the Canadian trilogy of our collective saga.[172]

That the researchers believe in their trilogy is made evident by this sentence. The saga has been written from a seeing that has been fashioned into a digestible opinion, a vision for policy in an allegorical writing that is considered suitable by the *Report* writers for their compatriots. But to write a policy report by employing features of allegory makes the *Task Force Report* a hybrid text: more than one writing strategy has been employed to produce an inviting meta-polis indicative of "what can come to be." If diverse readers can reach agreement about the importance of the *Report*'s vision, then it is hoped that they will also develop a single goal — the bringing to fruition and maintenance of Unity. Each particular reading occasion is supposed to become the site for allegiance to one cloth; Canada as the body of Unity and other emblems such as the flag, and personal and community histories, are all to be considered as one. Each particularity is asked to stop displaying unique colours and to instead weave itself into Canada's discursive flag of Unity.

The old, naive Canada, from the time before Unity, is presented as undergoing trials and tribulations. Canada can survive through perseverance and can in fact be purged, having endured a period of tremendous uncertainty.

The changes carry with them the promise of a future in
which the country and its people will come fully into their
own, seasoned by the years of trial and matured by challenges conquered. It is frequently out of such periods of torment and crisis as this that stronger countries are constructed.[173]

This patriot's progress saga is a form of allegory, and
allegorical narrative is the discursive structure that gives
form to the explanatory content of Task Force research.

Allegory makes an appeal to an almost scientific curiosity
about the order of things. The pilgrim's progress is a kind
of research project, taking all life as its boundaries. . . . The
protagonist is a conquistador; he arbitrates order over
chaos by confronting a random collection of people and
events, imposing his fate.[174]

The solution to the crisis of Canada involves restoring
order, and the restoration is to be achieved by reading the
body of Unity. Such a reading involves many levels of agreement, not the least of which is the production of consensus
after developing the need for a special type of battle in order
to fend off chaos. Chapter Eight makes clear that diagnostic
sensitivity, in a struggle for progress, is a form of battle. The
Task Force Report maintains the allegorical motif of the conflict body, which must be overcome. The confederate body is
too battle-weary to overtake the younger opponent; there
must be a strong protagonist who can surmount this obsta-
cle, and the hero will be the body of Unity. This abstract
symbol must not only overcome the conflict body and respect
the confederate body, it must also regulate bureaucracy. The
Unity body is not intended to be read as an anthropomorphi-
zation of bureaucracy, but as the collective effort of patriotic
people, for whom bureaucracy provides "essential" services.
The *Report* makes a continuous effort to keep bureaucracy
separate from the major characters (although each maintains a distinct relation to bureaucracy).[175] This separation is
produced by the repetition of form, of agency, and especially
of character description, as adjectives that name. For, "me-
tonomies are above all names, and are emphatically kept to
serve the needs of labelling and fixing the magical value of
whatever they are applied to."[176] The repetition of attributes

is a ritualized choral refrain within this symbolic saga, and also contributes to the maintenance of an anonymous style. Repetition heals the sin of fragmentation, produced by an unpatriotic self-interest. Allegorical writing can therefore project fragmentation: "When the allegorical author divides his [sic] major character into two antithetical aspects, he is bound to create doubled stories, one for each half. . . . They do not escape from their dualistic moral heritage."[177] "The doubling works with imagery instead of action, but otherwise presumably produces magical relations between the terms thus displayed in parallel."[178]

In the *Task Force Report*, the reader is invited to take up fragmentation of characterization as important to the plot of this version of Canada. The doubled body of conflict is written as corrupt, ill, and contagious. The so-called anorexic, independent-thinking disease has spread to portions of the confederate body. Both body concepts are walled off and written as pertaining to a Canada about to pass away. The future country has no rebellious ethnic disease; the pregnancy of pluralism and separatism, written as a disease that has used anxious and confused citizens as its hosts, is external to the invincible body of Unity.

> The contagion may be walled in, instead of walled out. . . .
> Allegory is thus not committed either . . . to a good or an evil place of isolation; it can designate either an interior or an exterior plague, depending upon the author's confidence about the world he inhabits.[179]

To wall off the body of conflict requires careful (patriotic/anonymous) reading. "[We] also share the conviction that constitutional change that is not predicated on a careful reading of the current crisis could easily undermine rather than enhance Canadian unity."[180] The careful reading must not be contextural; it must retain the characters as narrated, and their positions in relation to the crisis-at-hand:

> What we have been speaking about in the last few pages is the possible collapse of our country. Very few countries dissolve themselves in an atmosphere of sweet reason; economic hardship, social turmoil and violence almost always accompany changes of this magnitude and, whatever their

positive achievement, such changes commonly leave behind them a legacy of failed dreams and shattered hopes.[181]

In this, the climax of the *Report*, an impending, apocalyptic vision is presented, one of "hardship," "turmoil," "violence," and "shattered dreams." There is an antidote, however. Disaster can be averted by Canadians who wish to do their patriotic duty, each of whom will have to muster "a strong desire to commit oneself to some projects and purposes that are held in common among large groups of citizens."[182] In other words, a hopeful future can emerge out of a collective commitment to unity. Fletcher has written of allegory's power to create apocalyptic visions:

> Those final moments of vision which climax most allegorical works . . . are expressed by material elements which become traditional apocalytic images: the evildoers (dogs, sorcerers, whore-mongers, murderers, idolators, liars) are kept outside the walls of the Heavenly City. . . . The final apocalytic vision promises to mankind an eternal fruitfulness. It shows a triumph of love and creation, following the destructive war with evil, following the confession of sins and the saying of a creed.[183]

The sin to be confessed is that of "analysis," which accompanies too plural a focus; forgetting Ottawa has made persons across the country ethnically wayward, and vulnerable to the Quebec conflict-disease. To become strong patriots, citizens must choose the "right" image of Canada. Federal nationalism is supposed to be imagined, not as a cold and unfeeling bureaucracy, but in the form of a body: "the final apocalytic vision is taking its imagery from the simplest, most familiar source, namely the human body, the body of bodies. The body image need not be very obvious."[184] The giant social body of Unity, produced as a prescription, waits to come to life as the purveyor and container of consensus. Unity watches, waiting for further imitative movement from the Father-pen:

> But the very last words of this debate do not belong to us, they belong to you, our compatriots from the east and the west, from the north and the south. Now once again as we did, months ago, we are listening to all of you.[185]

6 *Misreading Nietzsche, Rewriting Bloom*

A contextural approach would cause sociologists interested in texts to hesitate to diagnose or rally to the call of the premature "we." Federal therapeutics are too polite to have any lasting impact. They pay lip-service to change, while working to serve the same institutional interests that they pretend to transcend. To turn away from this "we" requires a particular kind of selfishness, as a turning toward the very important yet highly devalued self, the self not organized or recognized in policy. In Anglo-Saxon, the word "self," spelled "selfe," was employed as a verb. It meant to depend on one's own judgment. Friedrich Nietzsche believed that intuition can be recognized in the images generated by the mind's eye. Recognition of such images would constitute the beginnings of another literacy—the ability to read oneself. "Whenever your spirit wants to speak in images, pay heed, for that is when your virtue has its origin and its beginning."[186]

Nietzsche's image-heeding is an important aspect of the reading activity which I have likened to weaving, the tendency to situate a reading question in a projection towards the remnants of kinship in any text. Technical reading and anonymous writing both seek a place to hide; they desire to linger as long as possible in immediate serviceability, and eventual stagnation. Gestural reading seeks a memory-place as merely a threshold, a place to move beyond. The longing for a monologic Unity is a deadly place to linger. Monologue is a textural surface to be surpassed. Projection is essential to gestural reading, which has a tendency to produce synesthe-

---

Notes to Chapter 6 are on p. 118.

sia in polyphonic perceptual stimulation and reading response. The ability to use more than one perceptual sense at a time (which is always already the case) can be used in reading as a self-conscious strategy that breaks down barriers to textural surfaces. Contextural misreading always seeks kinship. This turns both the written and reading into creative challenges.

My use of the term misreading is somewhat different from Bettelheim's, whose psychoanalytic work with young children revealed that their reading "problems" produced various slips of the eye. He understood the misreading of words as surface signals of underlying anxieties. His interest was in pointing out these anxieties to children and teachers, in order to help children stop misreading and become re-integrated into "normal" classroom reading habits. I would agree that misreading is a surface manifestation of deeper issues and influences. I have argued that these influences are only personal to the degree that the need for meaningful communication in authentic community could be called a personal problem. All reading and writing involves issues of kinship. When citizens assume that they will not be interested by what they may read in government policy documents, and/or assume that they will not comprehend even if they do try to read such documents, this indicates a problem. Media versions of government activity are privileged as quick and supposedly more "readable" summations of policy writing. In fact, much media coverage of government research is convoluted and obscures important issues. In some cases, it is completely off the mark. Yet citizens seem to prefer the media's confusion over their own reading. This indicates a tremendous lack of confidence in unique interpretive skills. It is for this reason that I advocate misreading. The lack of misreading indicates a suppression, both by individuals and by the state, of the many different voices through which creativity and intelligence speak. It is this suppression which is dangerous, not particular readings. The former kills the spirits of members; the latter nurtures them. Misreading is a creative act, an assertion of the reader's unique self. Bettelheim and Zelan's psychoanalytic study focusses on misreading as a cipher for many neurotic tendencies. I have always found it highly suspect that psychoanalysis has been eager to label creative activities as neurotic symptoms. It means very little to say that cultural production, in whatever form, is neurotic.

Harold Bloom has also explored misreading, though not explicitly his own. He is interested in how misreading overcomes influence to produce new maps of the mind: "what Blake and Wordsworth do for their readers, or can do, is closely related to what Freud does or can do for his, which is to provide both a map of the mind and a profound faith that the map can be put to saving use."[187] In his work *A Map of Misreading*, Bloom classifies misreading readers into categories. The over-determined nature of his categories indicates Bloom's need to control readers, which supersedes his ability to understand reading. Categories cannot explain the infinite variation made possible by insightful reading. The categories generated by his literary criticism do not do justice to a misreader's complex creative processes.

The indigenous peoples of this country participate in a gestural reading of society, which is, by "Canadian" bureaucratic standards, marginal, variegated, and eclectic. But it is only by maintaining a strong commitment to such a reading that these people have been able to sustain what they have come to call their integrity, a name which defines their relation to the federal imagination. Their gestural reading, proceeding from wholly other ways of living in culture, and from frustration with the constricting standards of the federal, has been for natives an articulation of their consciousness as "its own unique brand." This uniqueness is fundamental to a reading that experiences kinship; kinship already presupposes that there are distinct others. The federal imagination is faced with a truly other in regard to natives. And the reverse is also true. The two different readings are disorienting. Each is radically other; yet it is the federal consciousness that is written. The federal gives itself permission to write, and, assuming the position of giver, then gives the native peoples permission to read. The permission subsumes the other into part of the "we." This is the premature we, that erases the particular reader with anonymous writing.

The native case is only one example of the regulation and attempted erasure of alternate readings. Each reader is wholly other. Each brings a history, a physical and emotional context, as well as a distinctive curiosity to particular reading occasions. Correct or preferred reading suppresses unique offerings, rendering all misreading unproductive and faulty from the standpoint of federal ideology. Anonymous writing is a function of social control.

Policy, which attempts to control how it is read, can be said to try to police the imagination. The success of such writing — the degree to which the thought of readers may be influenced — depends on many factors. As Bruce Curtis has pointed out, one key factor is education. The degree to which the state's version of literacy is successful is to be judged by the degree to which readers mistrust their own judgment and stifle their thought. Literate patriots, in the worst version of the Task Force's unified Canada, would be those who only produce "correct readings," not because this would be all that they were capable of: rather because, in being loyal, this is all that they would want to think of doing. Such a grouping would constitute a squadron of citizens as civil servants whose eye movements would always be dictated by policy precedent.

Contextural analysis sees reading as an occasion to think otherwise, to read in a plural, textural manner. This requires keeping all of one's perceptive organs at the ready. It is advantageous, for example, to both read and hear a text at the same time. Bakhtin heard the texts of Rabelais and Dostoyevsky, and experienced the characters offered in these works as calling out to him. Their speeches were analyzed by him in terms of their voices. The ability to produce multilayered readings approximates what Bakhtin called the dialogical relation. Relations are dialogical when two voices hear and respond to the otherness of each. The critical reader can find such voices, even in the most anonymous of writings, as long as one's reading practices have not become estranged. As Greg Nielsen observed in his research on Quebec society, "given that all discourse is conceived in relation to the anticipated, albeit implicit, response and comprehension of the internalized other, one may discern an interior dialogical form in even the most monological speech genres."[188]

The strengthening of the perceptual dexterity of reading skills is not merely an academic exercise, for it is important to hear the voices of those whose interests may be pushed to the background. In the *Task Force Report*, for example, the blossoming of Quebec culture is rewritten so as to be almost unrecognizable. Nevertheless, this and other rewritings have not eliminated the blossom.

My reading of *The Report of the Task Force on Canadian Unity* has focussed upon (1) the organization of literary strategies for the production of social bodies, (2) the attempted co-ordination of plural communities into a new image of Canadian unity, and (3) the attempt to appropriate the reader's vision by engaging symbols in the text which invite reader-citizens to rethink Canada along the lines introduced in this rewriting. Instead of speaking of the plural, a patriot will speak of the "regions." Instead of thinking of Canadian "dualism," the reader is instructed instead to think about "unity." For a reader to be led to such an interpretation means that (s)he has fallen into a guided, linear reading in the manner examined by Morrison.

Yet, as my analysis shows, unique voices can be gathered up in reading without reifying their dynamics. A reader can listen to Quebec and to ethnic and indigenous peoples when one is not overwhelmed by the allegorical force of the iconic characters produced in the *Report*. These are the decorative features of absence, and the absence is constituted by the postponement of a relationship that is always promised but never forthcoming. Any relationship involves the exploration of the distinctive features of two or more participants. Letters appear but never their writer(s), who remain hidden behind what is documented, a covert strategy which attempts to contort writing into a taken-for-granted form of disclosure. Nevertheless, writing always reveals more than any author might wish.

My particular reading shows that there is no reason to lose hope. The pen need not always render the writer impotent. It is still possible to produce fertile reading and writing, as long as one is an assertive reader, always seeking to avoid anonymity.

Afterword

Patriotism is an attitude. It is a state of mind which cannot be worn and discarded like a cloak. In rereading some of the media's renditions of the Task Force's work, I am reminded of an interview which Marshall McLuhan gave to *Maclean's* in 1977 in which he stated that

> the effect of information is not to pull people together. It makes people feel independent when information is available everywhere. Everybody feels that they are able to make it alone. This is maybe an illusion but it happens at the speed of light, which is electric speed. Every place in the world is pulling away from every other place.[189]

An interview with Trudeau had been featured in *Maclean's* two months earlier in which he said, "The more frightened people are, the greater the problems seem, the more the world and Canadian economy are threatened, the more the values of children change in relation to those of their parents, the more we should regroup around the leader of the tribe."[190] Trudeau thought that he was the leader of the tribe, but McLuhan might have argued that it was Coca-Cola. In a world where the media are trusted by millions as the producers not only of goods but also of values, governments now use sophisticated advertising strategies in an effort to instill a sense of nationhood in their citizens. The US and Japan have been very successful in producing and maintaining strong patriots, but is this not because they are the homes of the majority of the world's mega-corporations, so that corporate and cultural ideologies can work jointly, using the same marketing strategies? To be literate one need not only be able to listen and/or to read, but one must also be able to remember. The media strategies only work when they help one to forget. I have to forget what I just saw in order to

---

Notes to the Afterword are on p. 118.

get on to the next, the newest, the latest item. Perhaps this explains why Canadians are so bored with constitutional talks and policy-making. Advertising, in order to be persuasive, has to create a certain alluring magic. Magic in media terms means making something radically new happen. In Canada, the man with the magic is the one who was able to break down policy discussion. Elijah Harper knows powerful magic. He can bring Parliament to a halt on camera. He can clog the writing machine. His magic is powerful because he will use modern parliamentary procedures and post-modern technologies to strive for a tribal consensus. It took an Elijah Harper to turn the media upside-down. He captured the attention of journalists in order to remind the world of the tribal concept of consensus.

Canadians are resistant citizens. This is not new. The *Task Force Report* calls this resistance apathy, and blames it on outmoded institutional practices and policies which need to be updated. Citizens have long had to deal with the policies brought forward by representatives. There is no suggestion in the *Task Force Report* of policy-makers or politicians adjusting to citizens. Philip Resnick has noted that

> there is not a single reference in the text of the *BNA Act* to the people, to democracy, or to what might be called popular sovereignty. There is a good deal about the Crown, about the Senate, about the Commons, about the division of power between federal and provincial governments, but the people as such do not figure at all.[191]

Resnick calls on the people to propose and promote something other than what we live with now — a new union rather than an uneven melding of what he calls the two "sociological nations" — English Canada and Quebec. All authors writing about Canadian social and political issues in recent times agree that popular support for constitutional issues is extremely difficult to rally. Roger Gibbins has described the collective mood as resistant to negotiation, indifferent, suspicious, and occasionally nasty.[192] These are all qualities which typify a state of ambivalence, wherein the citizen will not commit to anything. One cannot commit when what is being asked does not conform to what one needs. It can be extremely difficult to decide what one needs,

especially when pressure is brought to bear on all sides —
from media, government, work, and home. Everyone else
wants to decide what each person most needs. This can lead
to a sense of fatalism, as it has between citizens and politicians.

Edmund Morgan has investigated how early political representatives understood their roles in relation to their communities in his book *Inventing the People*. Representatives
chosen by specific constituencies came to see themselves as
representing the entire realm. "The people to whom they
attributed supreme power were themselves fictional and
could most usefully remain so, a mystical body, existing as a
people only in the actions of the Parliament that claimed to
act for them."[193] And

> the sovereignity of the people was an instrument by which
> representatives raised themselves to the maximum dis-
> tance above the particular set of people who chose them. In
> the name of *the* people they became all-powerful in govern-
> ment, shedding as much as possible the local, subject char-
> acter that made them representatives of a particular set of
> people.[194]

Perhaps the reason why Canadians cannot commit to any
of the constitutional proposals that have been brought forward is because they are keenly aware of a tremendous
degree of cultural tension which exists, but which has not as
yet been adequately identified or explained. Because I am a
document analyst, I explain such a tension as the interplay
of different texu(r)al surfaces. Writers have been trying to
explain this tension in relation to policy for more than two
centuries. In 1764 Thomas Pownall, then Governor of the
British Colonies in North America, wrote that

> the spirit of policy . . . of . . . the artificial or political state
> of these colonies becomes distinct from that which is . . .
> described as their natural state. The political state is that
> which policy labours to establish by a principle of repul-
> sion; the natural one is that state under which they actu-
> ally exist and move by a general common and mutual prin-
> ciple of attraction. . . . There must be some center of these
> composite movements, some lead that will predominate
> and govern in this general interest.[195]

Elijah Harper could well argue that the "centre" that can lead the nation(s) forward is his focus on consensus. This means seeking the wholehearted agreement of everyone. Is this why citizens continue to say "No!" although it fuels the so-called unity crisis? It seems to suit citizens better to sustain authentic indecision than to find a quick fix.

Appendix

Outlining *The Report of the Task Force on Canadian Unity*

Volume 1:
A Future Together: Observations and Recommendations

> How do we secure the fuller expression of duality in all the spheres to which it relates? How do we accommodate more satisfactorily the forces of regionalism that are altering the face of Canadian society? How do we make the principal of sharing an "operational value" in our country, and within and between our governments, so that duality and regionalism and the other features of Canadian life are given appropriate recognition?[196]

Chapter One: "Agenda for Change"

The mandate of this Task Force was to organize and represent what the members determined was a truly Canadian perspective on the state of the nation, as well as to publish the Task Force members' ideas on unity.

The Task Force began on 5 July 1977, with Jean-Luc Pépin (co-chair), John P. Robarts (co-chair), Gerald Beaudoin, Richard Cashin, Solange Chaput-Rolland, Muriel Kovitz, Ross Marks, and Ronald L. Watts. These eight men and women worked for 18 months, visiting 16 cities, and assessing public attitudes on the Canadian unity crisis. The *Report* states that they found their primary challenge to be coming from Quebec.

They recommend in this first chapter that beliefs and attitudes that are more "conducive to national unity" be encouraged through

---

The note to the Appendix is on p. 118.

"institutional and policy reform" (p. 4). Interventions such as educational programs and task forces are considered to be forms of
"rapid and determined response" which can help to ease and even
heal the crisis (p. 5). Canada is considered to be suffering, and citizens are encouraged to offer diagnoses. The ailment is first identified as a mental problem, "a diversity in ignorance of itself" (p. 6).
Diversity must be collected up. Citizens must learn to "cherish and
embrace it," to make an ally of diversity.

Chapter Two: "The Confederation Crisis"

The starting point of the Task Force's research is the historical
moment of the election of the PQ in 1976 (p. 11). The problems had
ripened "quietly beneath the surface" over a number of years until
election results and referendums showed themselves to be the rapidly surfacing symptoms of a serious illness. "Whatever one's preferences may be, the issue of Canadian unity will shoulder its way
to centre stage again and again during the next several years"
(p. 11). The members of the Royal Commission on Bilingualism and
Biculturalism saw this crisis coming in the 1960s. Duality combined with the impacts of modernization — "urbanization, industri-
alization, mass education, new modes of transportation and communications, and increasing secularization — have had a profound
impact on Quebec society, and on Canada as a whole" (p. 14). These
forces created two backlashes: (1) the bilingual backlash, as exem-
plified by the air traffic controller's strike in 1976, and (2) the push
for local autonomy. "To the fundamental challenge of Canadian
duality must now be added the other important challenge of Canadian regionalism" (p. 15). The native peoples became resentful of
the neglect they had long endured. Canadians in every sector re-
sented being continually told by the federal government that they
could obtain no more funds in an international economic climate of
restraint. And the federal government generally took on the
appearance of an impersonal bureaucracy becoming ever more
remote.

Nevertheless, this chapter ends on a high note. The crisis in
Canada can also be seen as "an opportunity to build anew" (p. 17).

Chapter Three: "The Anatomy of Conflict"

Concerns over duality and regionalism are elaborated. These are
described as being two different kinds of cleavages which need

more nurturing environments. Duality is defined as the co-existence of the two founding peoples of Canada as identified in the *BNA Act*.

The native peoples are very unhappy about being excluded. Yet no group is happy with the concept of duality. The English have difficulty thinking of two nations as one. French Canadians in Quebec feel that they are not "just" a branch of a larger French Canada. English-speaking Quebecers do not want to be any more closed off than they already are. All must face and learn to deal with the fact that from Quebec the distinct society has emerged, within which "[h]istory, language, law, common origins, feelings and politics, render Quebec at once a society, a province and the stronghold of the French Canadian people" (p. 25). French Canadians have been in Quebec for 300 years. They have kept the French language and legal system alive since 1866 in the form of the *Code Napoléon*. From their rich history, which they categorize as one of *survivance* (survival), they have developed a culture of *épanouissement* (blossoming).

Regionalism is defined as provincial differences and distinctiveness within English-speaking regions of Canada.

> The provincial political institutions are the primary frameworks through which regional populations can organize and express themselves, and their existence serves in turn to develop the social networks and interests based on them, thus reinforcing the provincial focus of regionalism (p. 27).

Chapter Three identifies five principal sources of diversity within English-speaking Canada:

1. Geography: There are many physical barriers which divide and separate parts of Canada.
2. History: Ties between regions have always been "tenuous" (p. 28). During the time of Vinland, the regions were considered to be separate islands. At the time of Confederation there were four provinces. Furthermore, people felt very strong loyalties to their respective provinces. "Loyalties to the province, which are particularly marked throughout Canada, antedate loyalty to the federation for English Canadians just as they do for French Canadians" (p. 29). Therefore people have tended to assess the achievements of the federation by the benefits extended to their respective provinces.
3. Economics: Provinces have unequal funds and unequal access to markets. They are also not equal in terms of resources and populations.

4. Ethnicity: Immigrants were not required to "mould" themselves to a common culture. They were, instead, invited to keep their cultures and languages of origin as long as they were committed to the concept of a unified Canada.
5. Federalism: The nation-state is a federation of provinces. The provinces oversee health care, social services, and education. The *BNA Act* gave the provinces these powers, thus reinforcing regionalism and strongly expressing the aspirations of the people in each province. "The provincial governments of many provinces in English-speaking Canada join the government of Quebec in calling the central government to account for its interventions in what they consider their own spheres of jurisdiction and for the more general treatment of the people of their province by federal authorities" (p. 31).

All of this has led to a crisis in which Quebec is identified as having stopped a dialogue.

Chapter Four: "Canada and the Search for Unity"

We attach value to both the English and French heritages. The "we" of the *Task Force Report* includes the members of the Task Force, writers, and "most of our countrymen" (p. 35).

The search for unity is described here as the search for a harmonizing of values, and a balance between provinces and the nation, minorities and the majority, as well as between native peoples and whites. The *Report* focusses on the notion of a common good as "a way of expressing the consensus that must support a free society" (p. 35). But in order to move towards a consensus people need to believe that they can receive what they consider to be their fair share of power and "the equitable distribution of benefits" (p. 36). What are the benefits available to all Canadians? We are not violent; ours is a "free and peaceful society" (p. 37). We are not starving. We have vast resources in the form of fresh water, forests, minerals, rich farmlands, and wide-ranging human resources. We have access to education and health services. Levels of income and shelter are of a high international standard in Canada as well. In light of all of this, the *Report* states that Canadians should pursue the three following social objectives: (1) Treat diversity as a resource and not as a problem. If we see our nation as a shelter, it only serves citizens who wish to be protected from economic and political change on the international and national levels. "The shelter theory only works domestically if the various communities in the country feel that by and large they have been given a fair shake" (p. 38). If community members feel exploited and/or neglected they will not make a commitment to a common good. Therefore injustices have to be rectified before citizens will make any such commitment. (2) Try to be more patriotic. Explore what the *Report* calls the "Canadian dimension," a form of patriotism based upon openness to diversity, the desire to make an imaginative contribution to Canada, and creative and productive co-operation within and between communities. "We also need to stimulate a consciousness on the part of the participating units in Canada that their local activities are likely to have a national aspect" (p. 39). (3) Politicians must adapt to necessary changes in the structure and functions of public institutions; such changes form a "natural and continuous process" (p. 40) of bureaucratic development. Chapter Four explains that no one answer will solve our problems. Action is required on many fronts. There will always be variability in terms of the sizes and strengths of our many communities. Political and legal structures must be open enough to permit progress. Thus it becomes essential to improve relations between provincial governments. In order to further clarify roles, the creation of new intergovernmental institutions is recommended.

Chapter Five: "Respecting Diversity"

The impersonal forces of modernization have had many impacts, including linguistic ones. "Modernization has brought strong pressure for linguistic assimilation to English" (p. 46). This is a source of resentment for Francophone Quebecois.

There is a Canadian language policy which was made statutory with the *Official Languages Act* of 1969, that declared French and English to be "equal in status, rights and privileges in all federal institutions" (p. 49). This declaration could not change social patterns unduly, however, and was seen by some as a compromise solution. Others did not support the language policy out of indifference.

The *Task Force Report* recommends that bilingual governmental services be a right guaranteed in the constitution. "Entrenchment should extend as well to the right of every person to have access to radio and television services in both the English and French languages and the availability in both official languages of all printed material intended for general public use" (p. 50).

The *Report* also supports Quebec's efforts to "ensure the predominance of the French language and culture in that province"

(p. 51). These aspirations have been essential to Canada since its beginnings and therefore must be pursued with confidence in order to secure Canadian unity.

Canada has an "enduring need for men and women who are fluently bilingual in French and English" (p. 54). Such people will take key positions in institutions and companies which are national in scope. And schools must keep pace. Schools should work harder to improve the availability of both official languages at all levels. "There is little doubt that federal financial incentives to support educational services to the English- and French-speaking minorities and for the teaching of the second official language have stimulated a number of provinces to provide more extensive and better quality educational services" (p. 54). But it is also time for provincial governments and minority communities themselves to support second-language programs and cultural activities. Federal funding should focus on cultural activities "with an interregional, national or international focus" (p. 54).

On the matter of Canadian ethnic pluralism, "[t]oday those of non-British or non-French origin represent more than a quarter of our population" (p. 55). There need be no conflict between duality and ethnic diversity, if pluralism can situate itself "within the framework of Canada's basic duality" (p. 55).

Immigration has been uneven geographically; therefore, ethnic patterns are not common across the nation.

> Yet the fact is that the members of the various ethnic groups have played a much more prominent role in the development of certain provinces and communities than of others, and in some their contribution has been a fundamental one. The regional or provincial framework is the one in which the various ethnic communities have been able to organize and express themselves most effectively and in which pluralism has become a living social reality (p. 55).

So the *Report* recommends that pluralism should be linked to regionalism. "Ethno-cultural organizations" should establish close ties with provincial governments to promote multiculturalism in the regions. And not just culture, but also equal access to services and equal opportunity should be developed and maintained.

On native issues, Chapter Five acknowledges that they are complex. Natives in Canada were made "a people" in the *BNA Act*, which gave Parliament jurisdiction over "Indians and their lands" (see Section 91 [24] *BNA Act*). Native rights are addressed in this *Report* as a long series of questions which go largely unanswered. "They will only be answered in the way the country's relationship with its first Canadians evolves in the next decade" (p. 57). Recommendations on native issues are made in the form of four possible "policy options": (1) Phase out special status, both constitutionally and in terms of special relationships with the government which have bred an "unhealthy dependence" and "neglect of their general welfare" (p. 57). (2) A modified federal role could give natives an option to stay on reserves, or move into white society. Such an option would require organizing all native assistance within one federal department with native civil servants in positions of major responsibility. This option is intended to "maximize the freedom of action of native people as individuals to choose a life in their traditional communities based on the land, or to enter the wider society with the greater confidence provided by the support put at their disposal" (p. 58). (3) Native sovereignty is considered the most "radical approach," since it involves creating more distance for natives from white society. Sovereignty here is defined as "the exercise of the principle of self-determination through the creation of autonomous institutions within the Canadian federal system." Under this option, natives would own their own lands and resources and make their own laws. Some see this as a way of recreating freedoms they enjoyed before Europeans arrived in Canada. (4) Combining aspects of the other options, natives would become "Citizens plus," meaning that they would be eligible for the regular benefits available to all Canadians from all levels of government and, in addition, to special benefits.

These options are followed by five recommendations. First, amend sections 11 and 12 of the *Indian Act* to ensure that native men and women gain or lose their status in precisely the same way. Second, promote and protect native languages and cultures more actively, and facilitate communication between natives here and indigenous peoples in other parts of the world. Third, pursue discussions with representatives of all native groups to arrive at "mutually acceptable" constitutional provisions. Fourth, take responsibility for natives in the areas of essential services, by entrenching their rights to these services in the constitution. Fifth, increase funding to natives for historical research, and see that they are adequately represented on boards that directly affect their interests.

Finally, Chapter Five tackles cultural policy. A distinction is made between culture defined as "high culture" or as "the complete fabric, values and life of a community" (p. 60). The *Report* gives preference to the second definition, saying that much of the responsibility for maintaining culture rests with the federal government. It is then suggested that the provincial governments take a more active role in cultural policy and development. "We would suggest that the central government should avoid extending its future operations into domains and pursuits which the provinces can and should perform for themselves" (p. 60). The federal government can give more prizes and continue to foster nationwide programs and nationally oriented groups, such as Katimavik and the National Youth Orchestra. The provincial governments should support and promote local and regional cultural activities and groups as a way to nurture and protect regional distinctiveness. Nowhere is the need to protect and nurture culture more apparent than in Quebec.

> The text of the constitution should ensure that the government of Quebec has the powers it requires to protect and develop its French heritage. Although the Task Force is of the opinion that the importance of this cultural domain in most provinces of English-speaking Canada is not yet as vital as it to Quebec, a constitution should make provision for the future (p. 61).

The *Report* encourages direct public participation in cultural activities, which it recommends should be promoted at the provincial level. Education in provincial societies and also in Canadian studies should be given greater attention.

All of this should be done in the interest of stability. "By adjusting Canada's policies and institutions to the needs of Canadian society as it develops, the citizens of this country can preserve a social equilibrium in the midst of rapid change" (p. 62).

Chapter Six: "Unity and the Health of the Economy"

The Canadian economy has always been sustained by exports.

> In the colonial 1840s, after the loss of preferential treatment in the British market, there was a movement in support of annexation by the United States. In the 1860s, the loss of reciprocity with the United States helped to forge the four colonies into an economic union which could withstand the pressures of annexation. In the depressed 1870s, the National Policy was designed to protect Canadian industries with tariffs (p. 65).

In this historical rendering, the federal "concentration of fiscal resources" is justified as a form of protectionism. Yet this concentration has produced interprovincial tensions which have intensified over time. The *Report* describes resources and commodities in terms of their value to the Canadian nation in its ongoing struggle to compete internationally. "In traditionally strong export markets for forestry products, minerals and other raw materials, Canada faces severe competition, primarily from the emerging states of the Third World" (p. 66). The implication is that provinces can only compete if they stay together and export on a unified basis.

> By operating within an integrated whole, regions can specialize in the production of goods and services in which they have a comparative advantage. At the same time, the possibility of interregional trade permits greater volumes of production, and hence lower costs. The size of the market in which the enterprises of a province, a region or a state can trade determines the limits of specialization (p. 67).

Seven forms of economic integration which best fit Canada's situation, according to the *Task Force Report* are outlined: free trade, customs union, common market, economic union, combined monetary and economic union, unitary states, and the federation. The federation is praised as a "substantially more complete form" (p. 68). It is more efficient; it is more effective in the public sector, setting interregional policies, borrowing from outside, constraining unfair competition between regions, and adjusting interregional transfer payments. "In a nutshell, integration creates a surplus, because the whole is greater than its parts. And the surplus, using the central government as an instrument, can be redistributed so that the strong parts help the weak to the benefit of the whole" (p. 69). Quebec in particular has stated that its grievances are not clearly understood or addressed by the federation. Other regions have expressed similar concerns. Yet the Task Force insists that the advantages of federal economic union far outweigh the disadvantages. Seven economic recommendations are outlined:

1. Section 121 of the *BNA Act* should be "clarified and strengthened" (p. 71). Section 121 states that "All Articles of the Growth, Produce, or Manufacture of any one of the Provinces shall, from and after the Union, be admitted free into each of the other Provinces" (Vol. 2, p. 90).
2. "We think that preferential purchasing policies should be permitted only in those cases where the province requires them to alleviate acute economic hardship" (p. 71).
3. Provinces make policies on professional activities which block job mobility. Thus, there should be more federal standards in this area. "We are aware that provincial legislation can impede the movement of capital, especially with regard to corporate mergers and the purchase of land. We think the constitution should expressly forbid such barriers" (p. 71).
4. The provinces should co-ordinate their tax regulations to prevent commercial competition for particular locations.

5. a) The conference of finance ministers should be used to develop countrywide consensus on the economy and co-ordinate forecasts.
   b) Conferences of first ministers on the economy should be held regularly, every two or three years. "The process of intergovernmental discussions might also be improved by allowing participation of business and labour groups" (p. 74).
6. Standardize economic opportunities by dividing provincial sources into ordinary and non-renewable resource revenues.

> Unlike the case for ordinary revenues, the second set of entitlements would be unrelated to the relative fiscal capacities of the provinces; rather these payments would be allocated according to some indicators measuring the degree in which provincial economies have experienced below average economic performance. They would be block grants for the purpose of encouraging economic development in provinces of relatively low rates of growth (p. 73).

7. a) Quebec's economy relies on trade with Canadian markets for manufactured goods which are not competitive internationally. Thus cutting "ties to Canada's customs union would profoundly disrupt Quebec's economy" (p. 74).
   b) The average income of francophones is lower than that of anglophone workers in the province of Quebec.
   c) Quebec's share of federal benefits has been steadily decreasing.
   d) How can Quebec be persuaded to stay in Canada? "We know that a country is not a business deal" (p. 76). Quebec has never gotten more than its fair share of benefits. Francophone Quebecers feel the costs of union deeply. Therefore they need to be persuaded with cogent arguments that they have more to lose than to gain by separation. "To this effect, we are convinced that the Canadian federation can be restructured and can achieve a better overall balance that would both suit and support a distinctive character for Quebec" (p. 77).

Chapter Seven: "A Restructured Federalism"

It is emphasized in the introduction that in both the western and eastern provinces of English-speaking Canada there is much criticism of the federal political system. The proposed solution is "a new Canadian constitution to meet the aspirations and needs of all the people of Canada" (p. 81).

Reworking of the constitution should proceed with these three objectives in the forefront: (1) central institutions should maintain and enhance the legitimacy of their positions as focal points for every group across the country; (2) regional and provincial needs, as well as requests for more automony, should be met with "greater institutional responsiveness" (p. 81); (3) Quebec deserves an "acceptable federalist response" to its grievances. A new constitution should be two official texts, one English and one French. It should (1) include a preamble declaring citizens' continuing "attachment to democratic institutions, federalism, human rights and the principle of supremacy of the law" (p. 81), (2) remember (i) the "historic partnership" between anglophones and francophones, (ii) Quebec's distinctiveness, (iii) the importance of the native peoples, and (iv) other cultural and regional groups, both in terms of the richness that their diversity brings to Canada and in terms of taking steps to develop and ensure equality of opportunity for all. All of this can be accomplished within a federal system, which is promoted in this chapter as being more accommodating of "desires for both unity and diversity," "more stable and more effective" (p. 82).

However, it is also argued that the federal system needs to be constitutionally restructured in six aspects:

1. Adjustment and redistribution of powers between Ottawa and the provinces, each having constitutional equality with the central government

   > We see the essential role and responsibilities of the central government as being to sustain, encourage and symbolize a Canadian identity and pride, to ensure the security and preservation of the Canadian federation, to have an overriding responsibility for the conduct of foreign policy, to oversee interprovincial and international trade, and to stimulate economic activity within the federation. . . . We see the essential role of the provinces as being to take the main responsibility for the social and cultural well-being and development of their communities, for the development of their economies and the exploitation of their natural resources, and for property and civil rights. . . . In the case of Quebec, it should be assured of the full powers needed for the preservation and expansion of its distinctive heritage (p. 85).

2. Federal-provincial relations should be handled by a "Council of the Federation composed of provincial delegates" (p. 83) instead of by the Senate.
3. Rework the Supreme Court and make it independent.
4. "Provision for constitutional amendment and flexibility" (p. 83).

5. Improve regional representation with electoral reform.

6. Entrench basic rights.

All of this can only be achieved if political leaders at all levels rise above particular interests and work "to achieve a spirit of creativeness and innovation, such as that which existed in the 1860s when out of political crisis and deadlock Confederation was conceived" (p. 84).

Quebec's distinctiveness must be entrenched in the constitution, but without giving it a special status. Two approaches are suggested: (a) Give Quebec law-making powers not available to other provincial jurisdictions since Quebec already has a system of civil law distinct from the other provinces, or (b) "allot to all provinces powers in the areas needed by Quebec to maintain its distinctive culture and heritage, but . . . do so in a manner which would enable the other provinces, if they so wished, not to exercise these responsibilities and instead leave them to Ottawa" (p. 87).

Federal constitutions allocate and list specific areas of legislative competence. The federal government and the provinces must agree on which subject matters are best handled by Ottawa or by each province. Chapter Seven provides seven categories to act as guidelines for the allocation of these powers. It is suggested that there should be "a list of exclusive central powers . . . a list of exclusive provincial powers . . . a list of concurrent powers with central paramountcy . . . a list of concurrent powers with provincial paramountcy . . . a limited list of those areas where central laws would be administered by the provinces . . . a limited list of those powers requiring joint action by Parliament and the provincial legislatures . . . a category of special overriding central powers with limitations specified" (p. 89). In addition, it is advised that residual power be assigned to the provincial governments.

A Systematic Functional Approach

Instead of following upon what Chapter Seven considers the "lack of coherence" evident in the *BNA Act*, it is suggested that policy areas be grouped under the general categories of contemporary government ministries and departments; for example, external affairs, defence, transportation, communication, health and welfare, environment. This is intended to provide logical and juridical clarity. Yet there are still grey areas. When it comes to matters such as resources, education and urban policies, all levels of government can rightly claim to have legitimate interests at stake. Conflicts in these areas can be managed in two steps, according to

Task Force writers: (1) review of policy areas with an eye towards defining and delineating these anew, and (2) the development of intergovernmental councils.

Taxing Powers

Broadly speaking, there are three approaches to the distribution of taxing powers. The first is to allocate specific sources of taxation to each order of government in terms of its perceived needs; the second is to retain all major tax resources in central hands with substantial unconditional transfers replacing provincial taxes; the third is to grant to both orders of government equal access to most revenue sources. . . . We favour the third approach (p. 92).

Overriding Central Powers

a) The Emergency Power

"When in future Ottawa seeks emergency powers it should be required to spell out the reasons in a proclamation, to obtain approval of the proclamation by both the House of Commons and the revised second chamber . . . as soon as is reasonably possible, and for a specified duration" (p. 93).

b) The Declaratory Power

This is the federal power to declare local works (such as pipelines) to be for the advantage of more than one province, or for the general advantage of all of Canada. Chapter Seven suggests that "the central declaratory power should be retained but that its use should be subject to the consent of the provinces concerned" (p. 93).

c) The Spending Power

In our opinion, the spending power must be retained to enable Ottawa to ensure unconditional equalization payments to the poorer provinces and to ensure Canada-wide standards for programs in which a strong general interest has been demonstrated. But we think it, too, should have limits. The exercise by Ottawa of its spending power, whenever it is related to programs which are of provincial concern, should be made subject to ratification by the reconstituted upper house which we are proposing [the revised second chamber]. To further safeguard provincial autonomy, provinces should have the right to opt out of any program and where appropriate receive fiscal compensation (pp. 93-94).

d) The Powers of Reservation and Disallowance

Provincial legislation can be blocked by the governor-general or the central cabinet. Lieutenant-governors can refuse to accept bills approved by provincial legislatures and hold them for consideration by the governor-general. And the federal cabinet can veto provincial statutes, if decided within a year. Chapter Seven advises that these two powers be eliminated.

e) The Power to Appoint Lieutenant-Governors

Let this be the responsibility of the Queen.

Federal-provincial relations need to be improved. The following courses of action are suggested.

i)   Acknowledge and promote co-operation between central and provincial governments, which are inevitably interdependent.
ii) Promote an already strong and adaptable executive federalism.
iii) Build this executive federalism into central parliamentary institutions via a new second chamber.
iv) A new second chamber of the federal parliament, as a council of provincial representatives (but not members of provincial parliaments), would be less problematic than an elected Senate, it is suggested, since its members would not be beholden to any specific constituency. A representative body is required, it is argued, which deals exclusively with intergovernmental issues.
v)   This new second chamber should be called the Council of the Federation. It would be composed of delegations from each province with voting rights and membership based upon provincial population. Central government ministers could sit in, but as non-voting members only.

> All this would be a radical departure, one that would end the traditional roles of the Senate as a chamber of "sober second thought" on Commons' legislation and as an investigatory body on various issues. These roles we would transfer to a strengthened committee structure in the Commons. Unlike the existing Senate, the Council of the Federation, whose structure, powers and functioning we have here only sketched out, would be an institution which could play a major part in ensuring that the views of provincial governments are taken into account before any central action which might have an impact upon areas of legitimate provincial concern occurs, thus inducing more harmonious federal-provincial relations (p. 99).

vi) The council of first ministers should run on an annual basis and this body should develop a new committee to deal specifically with intergovernmental policy issues, "we further recommend that a standing task force of officials and experts representing all governments be established to review policy and program duplication on a continuing basis" (p. 99). In addition, standing committees need to be established in all legislatures, both federal and provincial, to review major conference activities and agreements.

The Supreme Court

All supreme court justices are appointed by the federal government. A parliamentary statute established this court in 1875. The statute could be changed by Parliament. The Supreme Court's existence and independence should be established by entrenching its general appellate jurisdiction in a revised constitution. The composition of the court should be changed to 11 judges (5 civil, 6 common law) and three benches (one with provincial jurisdiction plus Quebec law section, one with federal juridiction and a third with constitutional jurisdiction), with a Chief Justice to be chosen from among the members of the court. Provincial judges should be appointed by provincial governments. In the case of higher courts, though, provincial governments should consult with federal officials.

Constitutional Change and Adaptation

Both provincial and federal levels of government must participate and negotiate on constitutional amendments. There are also somewhat more informal avenues for constitutional interpretation and alteration. "Judicial review, customs and conventions, and federal-provincial agreements are important means of change through which the constitution can evolve" (p. 102).

Formally, an amendment procedure should be contained in a revised constitution which concerns joint matters, and that allows for changing needs but that also secures assigned federal and provincial functions. "There are two distinct elements in an amendment formula: a definition of the subject matters which require both a central and a regional consensus; and the definition of that consensus itself" (p. 103). The approval of amendments could involve a simple majority vote in the House of Commons and the proposed second chamber. Ratification should be accomplished by means of a Canada-wide referendum process.

Each level of government should be allowed to delegate powers to the other with mutual consent "on condition that such delegations be subject to periodic revision and be accompanied where appropriate by fiscal compensation" (p. 104).

Electoral Reform

Chapter Seven recommends that the number of Commons seats be increased by 60. The additional seats should be filled by party members whose names are to be introduced on ranked lists before an election. In terms of party representation, "allocate the 60 seats on the percentage of the country-wide vote received by each party and apply what is known as the d'Hondt formula for allocating seats provincially among parties" (p. 106). The committee structure in the House of Commons needs to be strengthened by, (1) making the cabinet more accountable to the House, and (2) giving House committees the Senate's power to review and investigate through studies with an eye toward improving legislation.

Individual and Collective Rights

It is suggested that in a revised constitution, rights be grouped into three categories:

a) individual rights which include political, legal, egalitarian, and economic liberties;
b) collective rights of individuals by affiliation;
c) collective rights exclusive to groups.

And five forms of protection for rights are cited:

> (1) the precedents affirmed by the common law as declared by the courts; (2) simple acts or statutes passed by our legislatures; (3) a charter of human rights collected in a single statute; (4) embodiment in a portion of the constitution so that all government legislation must take them into account; and (5) embodiment in a portion of the constitution which is entrenched — that is, requires a special approval procedure for any change (p. 107).

Therefore key individual and collective rights must be entrenched in a revised constitution. And the Supreme Court's independence must be ensured to protect such rights. Specifically, individual legal, economic, political, language and native rights need to be entrenched in the Bill of Rights; it is also considered important to "limit the set of entrenched rights applying to both orders of government to those on which both central and provincial governments can agree now" (p. 109).

Canadian unity can only develop if there is "a radical modification to the existing federal system" (p. 109). And to maintain "unity within a political framework of divided power requires continued effort" (p. 109). The recommended revisions attempt to formally recognize diversity and secure individual and collective rights.

Chapter Eight: "A Future Together"

Task Force writers state in this concluding chapter that the crisis in Canadian unity is an opportunity. "It is frequently out of such periods of torment and crisis as this that stronger countries are constructed" (p. 113).

They affirm that Quebec has the right to settle its own destiny. Since it has established itself as a "distinct political community" this has more practical import than legal recognition and amendment. Quebec's right to secede must be respected as a necessary part of a democratic process. In addition, the rights of English-speaking Canadians must be respected. They also have the right to determine what would suit them best if Quebec decided to secede.

"English-speaking Canada does not speak with one, but with many voices, so they are sometimes difficult to hear, but our study and consultation do not lead us to believe that sovereignty-association as advanced would have great appeal in the other nine provinces" (p. 114).

It is easier to generate constitutional reform than to repair Canada. To unify Canada requires imaginative and sensitive action, not easy to implement. For this reason the observations and recommendations fall into two categories. The first category deals with restructuring the federal system. "The second category includes recommendations and observations which are not concerned so much with the restructuring of Canadian federalism as with the spirit which should underlie it and the practices which would give it life and movement" (p. 115).

What undermines constitutional reform?

> First, for several generations there has been a remarkably consistent and coherent constitutional point of view shared by a broad majority of French-speaking Quebecois. This has served both to support and to limit the freedom of action of Quebec's political leaders. No Quebec politician can afford to stray far from this collective will (p. 116).

Secondly, English-speaking Canadians have been apathetic about reforms. If constitutional amendment required regional voting across Canada, then citizens might have a reason to be interested. "Wide-ranging political agreement seems unlikely to be achieved without strong supporting consensus among the people generally, and we believe that citizens who are asked to declare themselves directly on a proposal are more likely to interest themselves in it than those who are not" (pp. 117-18).

This "collective saga" ends by reiterating the three principles of "duality, regionalism and the sharing of benefits" (p. 118).

Chapter Nine: "Specific Recommendations"

Seventy-five recommendations, most of which have already been outlined.

Appendix 1: Terms of Reference
Privy Council minutes from 5 July 1977, 24 August 1977 and 28 February 1978 which relate to the Task Force.

Appendix 2: The Role of the Task Force
This section outlines the mandate of the Task Force.

Volume 2
Coming to Terms: The Words of the Debate

This volume is a Canadian political and constitutional glossary for the layperson. It is divided into three parts, with two appendices. Part 1 is entitled "General Social and Political Terms" and contains the following six sections: (1) Societies and Communities; (2) Political Relationships and Organizations; (3) Rights, Liberties and Freedoms; (4) Forms of Government; (5) Federation, Confederation and Economic Association; and (6) Constitution. Part 2 is called "The Canadian System of Government" and includes: (1) Sources of the Canadian Constitution; (2) The Parliamentary Form of Government; (3) The Canadian Federal System; (4) The Protection of Fundamental Rights; and (5) Territorial and Local Governments. Part 3 suggests "Options for the Future" under: (1) Constitutional Frameworks; (2) Basic Options and Variations; (3) Sovereignty-Association; and (4) Federal Options. Finally there are Appendix I: Historical Documents, and Appendix II: Proposals from Official Groups and Private Organizations.

Volume 3:
A Time to Speak: The Views of the Public

This volume is an edited selection of comments made by individuals and groups that addressed the Task Force. The excerpts have been categorized into five parts and 20 chapters that also contain interpretive summaries and conclusions. Part I, The Communities, contains seven chapters: (1) The Founding Peoples; (2) The Official Languages; (3) The Native Communities; (4) The French Communities outside Quebec; (5) The English Community in Quebec; (6) The Other Ethnic Groups; and (7) The Regional Communities. Part II, The Search for Identity, is broken down into Chapters 8-11: (8) Identities and Cultures; (9) Education; (10) The Media; and (11) Symbols. Part III, Quebec, is divided into: (12) A Disaffected Province, and (13) The Sovereignty-Association Option. Part IV, Economic, contains three chapters: (14) Governments and the Economy; (15) Regional Economies; and (16) Resources. Part V, Politics and the Constitution, has four chapters: (17) The Distribution of Powers; (18) Regional Representation in Central Institutions; (19) Protection of Fundamental Rights; and (20) Means of Constitutional Change. There are five appendices as well: A: Terms of Reference; B: The Role of the Task Force; C: Comments on the Task Force; D: Individuals and Groups Presenting Briefs; and E: Regional Organizing Committees.

Notes

1. Caws, *The Eye in the Text: Essays in Perception, Mannerist to Modern*, p. 10.
2. Ibid., p. 11.
3. Newman, "The Good News from Robarts and Pepin: Canada, the Uncountry, Can Be Reinvented," p. 3.
4. Lyotard, *The Inhuman*, p. 27.
5. Ibid., p. 26.
6. *The Report of the Task Force on Canadian Unity*, 1: 142. Hereafter cited as the *Task Force Report*.
7. Hon. J. Clark, *An Invitation to Help Build a Better Canada / Une invitation à batir ensemble l'avenir du Canada*, p. 8.
8. *The American Heritage Dictionary of the English Language*, p. 288. Hereafter cited as *Dictionary*.
9. *Task Force Report*, 1: 28.
10. Ibid., p. 95.
11. Ibid., p. 41.
12. Samuel R. Levin, "Allegorical Language," pp. 24-25.
13. Clifford, *The Transformations of Allegory*, pp. 14-15.
14. Green, *Knowing the Poor: A Case Study in Textual Reality Construction*, p. 63.
15. Morrison, "Some Properties of 'Telling-Order Designs' in Didactic Inquiry," pp. 245-62.
16. Ibid., p. 247.
17. Green, *Knowing the Poor*, p. 18.
18. Curtis, "The Speller Expelled: Disciplining the Common Reader in Canada West," pp. 346-68.
19. Smith, "The Active Text: A Textual Analysis of the Social Relations of Public Textual Discourse," p. 8.
20. Chua, "Democracy as a Textual Accomplishment," p. 541.
21. O'Neill, *Essaying Montaigne: A Study of the Institution of Reading and Writing*, pp. 98-99.
22. Ibid., p. 62.
23. Derrida, *Of Grammatology*, pp. 314-15.
24. Alex McHoul, *Telling How Texts Talk: Essays on Ethnomethodology*, pp. 125-26.
25. Ibid., p. 137.
26. Mitchell, *The Process of Reading: A Cognitive Analysis of Fluent Reading and Learning to Read*, p. 6.
27. Ibid., p. 34.
28. On potential dynamics of pleasure in textuality, see Roland Barthes's *Le Plaisir du Texte* (Paris: Seuil, 1973). Also important is his essay "From Work to Text" in *Textual Strategies*, ed. Josue V. Harari, pp. 73-81.
29. Mitchell, *The Process of Reading*, p. 101.
30. Bleich, *Readings and Feelings: An Introduction to Subjective Criticism*, p. 4.

31. Bettelheim and Zelan, *On Learning to Read: The Child's Fascination with Meaning*, p. 101.
32. Ibid., p. 102.
33. Mitchell, *The Process of Reading*, p. 125.
34. Bakhtin, *Problems of Dostoyevsky's Poetics*, p. 251.
35. Ibid., p. 237.
36. Ibid., p. 252.
37. Norman Holland, *Poems in Persons*, p. 145.
38. Ibid., p. 100.
39. Holland, *5 Readers Reading*, p. 18.
40. Ibid., p. 13.
41. Fish, *Is There a Text in This Class? The Authority of Interpretive Communities*, p. 52.
42. Ibid., pp. 319-20.
43. Ibid., p. 355.
44. Brain, *The Decorated Body*, p. 92.
45. Leach, "The Big Fish in the Biblical Wildernness," p. 139.
46. Tyler, "Ethnography, Intertextuality and the End of Description," p. 83.
47. Ibid., p. 95.
48. Leitch, *Deconstructive Criticism: An Advanced Introduction*, p. 186.
49. Ibid., p. 95.
50. Foucault, "What is an Author?" pp. 159-60.
51. Department of the Secretary of State, *The Canadian Style: A Guide to Writing and Editing*, p. 199.
52. See Charles Bazerman's "What Written Knowledge Does: Three Examples of Academic Discourse," pp. 361-87. An example of the activity of scientific discovery can be found in Harold Garfinkel, et al., "The Work of a Discovering Science Construed with Materials from the Optically Discovered Pulsar," pp. 131-58. On what comes to constitute knowledge in sociology, see Dorothy Smith's "The Ideological Practice of Sociology," pp. 39-54.
53. *Task Force Report*, 1: 3.
54. Ibid.
55. See Thomas Hobbes, *Leviathan*. Hobbes's introduction provides a summary of some of his images concerning the body of "that great Leviathan called a Common-Wealth, or State" (p. 81); see also Auguste Comte's *A General Theory of Positivism*. Chapter 6 contains many references to society as a "she," a "Supreme Being" by the name of "Humanity."
56. See Dorothy Smith, "The Active Text."
57. See Bakhtin, *Problems of Dostoyevsky's Poetics*, pp. 73, 11, and 147. Bakhtin might describe the *Task Force Report*'s perceptual conflict as operating within a struggling, fragmented, floating discourse seeking a dialogue which never emerges. He could then append my appropriation of his category, saying that I am not discussing dialogue on the threshold, but a threshold seeking dialogue.
58. *Task Force Report*, 3: 10. My example of one citizen's analysis is only one of many which I could have chosen. Volume 3 of the *Report* contains "data" from the hearings in a supposedly raw form. This data is then worked up into a diagnosis in Volume 1. The choice and positioning of comments in Volume 3 makes them appear random, when this is probably not the case. However, an investigation of the implications of this aspect of the research behind the Report would be a project ample enough for at least one other thesis.
59. *Task Force Report*, 1: 5.
60. Ibid.

61. Ibid.
62. Ibid.
63. The patriot as a component of the social body was articulated by Comte thus: "The people represent the activity of the Supreme Being, as women represent its sympathy, and philosophers its intellect" (ibid., p. 414).
64. *Task Force Report*, 1: 11.
65. Ibid., pp. 12-13.
66. Ibid., p. 13.
67. Ibid., p. 15.
68. Ibid.
69. Ibid., p. 16.
70. Ibid.
71. Edmund Leach, *Social Anthropology*, p. 60. A stranger threatens habitual thought and actions. (S)he knows an alternate everday reality to one that would be recognized as familiar among friends. There are at least two different ways to deal with the threat: (a) make the other into a weirdo whose differences are idiosyncratic deformations of inconsequential or detrimental value, or (b) know that the other threatens taken-for-granted values and that the threat can be taken up as a constructive challenge, as an opportunity to learn something new. Nonetheless, Leach's anthropological experience lends a valuable insight to the study of dyadic relations between groups as well as between individuals.
72. *Task Force Report*, 1: 24. The double imagery of the grotesque is at work in this representation. Bakhtin states that the grotesque image "is organically combined on the one hand with swallowing and devouring, on the other hand with the stomach, the womb, and childbirth." The *Report*'s devouring body is the Romanesque "bureaucracy that exacts tribute from its subjects and gives little in return," while the "blossoming" body of Quebec experiences itself as pregnant. The report rejects outright both of these images, and produces an allegorical reversal in its articulation of (1) the federal government as a caring agency, and (2) its diagnosis of Quebec as being misguided; the Report examines Quebec's stomach, and diagnoses it as being sick with self-indulgence. The grotesque social body is employed in Task Force writing to identify a former partner as ill, so different and distant that it now appears to be a kind of stranger. See Mikhail Bakhtin, *Rabelais and His World*, trans. Helene Iswolsky (Bloomington: Indiana University Press, 1984), p. 339.
73. *Task Force Report*, 1: 28.
74. See Derrida, *Otobiographies: L'enseignment de Nietzsche et la politique du nom propre*.
75. *Task Force Report*, 1: 6.
76. Ibid., p. 26.
77. Ibid., p. 27.
78. Ibid., p. 26.
79. Ibid, p. 27.
80. Morrow, "Critical Theory and Critical Sociology," p. 730. Critical theorists have not written of style as it concerns me here in the present analysis. However, Adorno has described Heidegger's philosophy as primarily laden with "jargon." "The jargon of authenticity is ideology as language without any consideration of specific content." In *The Jargon of Authenticity* (p. 160), the conceptual distance between "jargon" and "style" is not vast. However Adorno's understanding of jargon retains the ideology of "specific content" and segregates this from language in a way which style does not.

81. Here I am employing one of Derrida's insights which pertains to writing as the "disruption of presence in the mark." This appears in his essay "Signature Event Context" (*Margins of Philosophy*, p. 327).
82. *Task Force Report*, 1: 6.
83. Ibid., p. 31.
84. *Task Force Report*, 3: 6.
85. Bakhtin's understanding of the voice is elaborated throughout his work *The Dialogic Imagination*. There is a clear definition and descrption of automatic writing in James's *The Principles of Psychology*, pp. 393-401.
86. See the *Task Force Report* ("Coming to Terms," p. 10), for the definition of the term dualism as used throughout the Report.
87. Bakhtin, *Problems of Dostoyevsky's Poetics*, p. 213.
88. Ibid., p. 217.
89. de Tocqueville, *Democracy in America*, p. 695.
90. *Task Force Report*, 1: 11.
91. de Man, *Allegories of Reading*, p. 131.
92. *Task Force Report*, 1: 41.
93. Ibid., p. 35.
94. Ibid., p. 36.
95. See Bakhtin's *Problems of Dostoyevsky's Poetics*, p. 233.
96. *Task Force Report*, 1: 41.
97. Malinowski, *Magic, Science and Religion and Other Essays*, p. 146.
98. *Think Canadian*, p. 2.
99. *Task Force Report*, 1: 37.
100. de Man, *Allegories of Reading*, p. 67.
101. Ibid., p. 109.
102. *Task Force Report*, 1: 37-38.
103. Simmel, *The Sociology of Georg Simmel*, p. 149.
104. Derrida, *The Ear of the Other: Otobiography Transference Translation*, p. 36.
105. *Task Force Report*, 1: 45.
106. Ibid., p. 46.
107. Ibid., p. 49.
108. Ibid., p. 50.
109. Ibid., p. 52. The role of the provincial government as a critical agent as set out in this *Report* does articulate a bureaucratic precedent wherein the federal discourse can appear to lose strength, but may not necessarily do so. Provincial discourse may indeed become fractal (a recursive version of the federal discourse), a smaller, though equally potent form of unity-thought.
110. Comte, *General View of Positivism*, pp. 400-401.
111. *Task Force Report*, 1: 55.
112. Ibid.
113. *Task Force Report*, 1: 55-56.
114. Melnyk, *Radical Regionalism*, p. 17.
115. *Task Force Report*, 1: 56.
116. Ibid. All phrases quoted in this paragraph are to be found on p. 57.
117. Ibid., p. 58.
118. Ibid.
119. Ibid., p. 59.
120. Ibid.
121. Ibid., p. 60.
122. Ibid.
123. Ibid., p. 61.

124. Ibid., p. 62.
125. Ibid.
126. Ibid., p. 65.
127. Chua, "Democracy as a Textual Accomplishment," p. 546. And as Dorothy Smith has explained: "The institutional language (underlined in the figure) knits the description directly into the mandated course of action. The particulars and the interpretive schema they intend are a seamless cloth (from "The Active Text," p. 45). Her "institutional ethnographic" type of document analysis works best with texts or portions of texts which have been read anonymously. It is not sufficient for analyzing anonymous grammars. "All writing . . . in order to be what it is, must be able to function in the radical absence of every empirical addressee in general" (as stated by Derrida, *Margins of Philosophy*, pp. 315-16).
128. *Task Force Report*, 1: 65.
129. Ibid., pp. 66-67.
130. Ibid., p. 68.
131. Ibid., p. 69.
132. Ibid., p. 70.
133. Ibid., p. 32. The *Report*'s "greater question excludes any possibility for discussion of Quebec nationalism. Canadians were told to address themselves to the greater question of "nationhood"—one country stretching from sea to sea—with all of its peoples sharing a "common allegiance to the development of a greater Canada" (p. 133).
134. Turner, *The Body & Society*, p. 93.
135. Ibid., p. 185.
136. The parasite-host trope is a deconstructive turn employed especially by Derrida, Miller, and Serres. The concluding section of Gregory Ulmer's article "The Object of Post-Criticism" provides a concise review of this turn in relation to the text and the critic. See *The Anti-Aesthetic: Essays on Postmodern Culture*, pp. 83-110.
137. *Task Force Report*, 1: 71.
138. Ibid., p. 72.
139. Ibid., p. 74.
140. Ibid.
141. Ibid., p. 75.
142. Ibid., p. 76.
143. Ibid., p. 84.
144. Ibid. All quotations in the preceding paragraph as well as this citation have been extracted from 1: 85.
145. Ibid., p. 81.
146. Ibid., p. 87.
147. Ibid., p. 88.
148. Ibid., p. 89.
149. Chua, "Democracy as a Textual Accomplishment," p. 541.
150. *Task Force Report*, 1: 87.
151. Ibid.
152. Ibid., p. 91.
153. Ibid., p. 95.
154. Ibid., p. 96.
155. *Task Force Report*, 3: 127.
156. O'Neill, *Five Bodies*, p. 27.
157. Ibid., p. 51.

158. Ibid., p. 67.
159. Turner, *The Body & Society*, p. 177.
160. O'Neill, *Five Bodies*, p. 117.
161. Langland, *Piers Plowman*, p. 85.
162. Machiavelli, *The Prince and the Discourses*, pp. 41-42.
163. For more on this subject, see Jacques Le Goff, *The Medieval Imagination*; Andrew Tomasello, *Music and Ritual in Papal Avignon, 1309-1403*; and W. Godzich and S. Spadaccini, *Literature among Discourses*. Also fascinating are the "lays" of Marie de France; she transcribed many courtly minstrel songs, and at the same time reshaped them into romantic prose. See her *French Medieval Romances*.
164. Langland, *Piers Plowman*, p. 74.
165. Leach, *Culture and communication*, pp. 71-72.
166. Le Goff, *The Medieval Imagination*, p. 160.
167. Fletcher, *Allegory: The Theory of a Symbolic Mode*, p. 161.
168. Ibid., p. 105.
169. [N.a.] *Everyman and Other Religious Plays*, p. 25.
170. *Task Force Report*, 1: 114-15.
171. Ibid., p. 118.
172. Ibid., p. 113.
173. Ibid., p. 69.
174. Fletcher, *Allegory*, p. 69.
175. In Kerr, *English Literature / Medieval*, there are a number of interesting descriptions of allegory's tendencies to separate realms of meaning. For example, "In *Piers Plowman*, there is as much knowledge of life as in Bunyan; but the visible world is only seen from time to time" (p. 195); "though there is a double meaning, there are not two separate meanings presented one after the other to the mind. The signification is given along with, or through, the scene and the figures (p. 186).
176. Fletcher, *Allegory*, p. 161.
177. Ibid., p. 185.
178. Ibid., p. 186.
179. Ibid., p. 214.
180. *Task Force Report*, 1: 115.
181. Ibid., p. 114.
182. Ibid.
183. Fletcher, *Allegory*, pp. 354-55.
184. Ibid., p. 357.
185. *Task Force Report*, 1: 118.
186. Nietzsche, *Thus Spoke Zarathustra*, p. 101. Also see the *Dictionary of Archaic and Provincial Words* for former meanings and variant spellings of "selfe."
187. Bloom, "The Internalization of Quest-Romance," p. 3.
188. Nielsen, "Reading the Quebec Imaginary: Marcel Rioux and Dialogical Form," p. 135.
189. McLuhan, "Interview," p. 4.
190. Trudeau, "Interview," pp. 4-5.
191. Resnick, *Toward a Canada-Quebec Union*, p. 92.
192. Gibbins, "Constitutional Politics in the West and the Rest," p. 22.
193. Morgan, *Inventing the People*, p. 49.
194. Ibid., p. 50.
195. Pownall, *The Administration of the British Colonies*, p. 7.
196. *Task Force Report*, 1: 141. The rest of the references are indicated by page references in the text of the Appendix.

Bibliography

Adorno, Theodor. *The Jargon of Authenticity*. Translated by K. Tarnowski and F. Will. Evanston, IL: Northwestern University Press, 1973.

American Heritage Dictionary of the English Language, The. New York: American Heritage/Houghton Mifflin, 1969.

Anderson, H., and G. Anderson, eds. *An Introduction to Projective Techniques*. Englewood Cliffs, NJ: Prentice-Hall, 1951.

Anthi, Per Roar. "Non-Verbal Behavior and Body Organ Fantasies: Their Relation to Body Image Formation and Symptomatology." *The International Journal of Psychoanalysis* 67 (1986): 417-28.

Austin, John L. *How to do Things with Words*. London: Oxford University Press, 1962.

————. "Other Minds." In *Logic and Language* (Second Series), edited by A. Flew, pp. 123-58. Oxford: Basil Blackwell, 1961.

————. *Philosophical Papers*. London: Oxford University Press, Clarendon Press, 1961.

————. *Sense and Sensibilia*. Edited by G. Warnock. London: Oxford University Press, 1962.

Bakhtin, Mikhail. *The Dialogic Imagination*. Edited by Michael Holquist and translated by Caryl Emerson and Michael Holquist. Austin, TX: University of Austin Press, 1981.

————. *Problems of Dostoyevsky's Poetics*. Edited and translated by Caryl Emerson. Minneapolis: University of Minnesota Press, 1984.

————. *Rabelais and his World*. Translated by Irene Iswolsky. Bloomington: Indiana University Press, 1984.

Barthes, Roland. "From Work to Text." In *Textual Strategies: Perspectives in Post-Structuralist Criticism*, edited by J. Harari, pp. 73-81. Ithaca, NY: Cornell University Press, 1979.

————. *Mythologies*. Translated by Annette Lavers. London: Granada Publishing, 1973.

————. *Le plaisir du texte*. Paris: Seuil, 1973.

Baudrillard, Jean. *In The Shadow of the Silent Majorities ... or The End of the Social*. Translated by P. Foss, et al. New York: Semiotext(e), 1983.

————. *Simulations*. Translated by P. Foss, et al. New York: Semiotext(e), 1983.

_____. *Le système des objets: la consommation des signes*. Paris: Gallimard, 1968.

Bazerman, Charles, "What Written Knowledge Does: Three Examples of Academic Discourse." *Philosophy of the Social Sciences* 2 (1981): 361-87.

Benjamin, Walter. *Illuminations*. Edited and introduced by H. Arendt and translated by H. Zohn. New York: Schocken, 1969.

Berger, Harry Jr. "Bodies and Texts." *Representations* 17 (Winter 1987): 144-66.

Bettelheim, Bruno, and Karen Zelan. *On Learning to Read: The Child's Fascination with Meaning*. New York: A. A. Knopf, 1982.

Bleich, David. *Readings and Feelings: An Introduction to Subjective Criticism*. Urbana, IL: National Council of Teachers of English, 1975.

Bloom, Harold, ed. *Romanticism and Consciousness: Essays in Criticism*. New York: W. W. Norton, 1970.

Bloomfield, Morton, ed. *Allegory, Myth and Symbol*. Cambridge, MA: Harvard University Press, 1981.

Blum, Alan. "Positive Thinking." *Theory and Society* 1, 3 (Fall 1974): 245-69.

_____. *Theorizing*. London: Heinemann, 1974.

_____, and Peter McHugh. *On the Beginning of Social Inquiry*. London: Routledge & Kegan Paul, 1974.

Brain, Robert. *The Decorated Body*. New York: Harper & Row, 1979.

Bunyan, John. *The Pilgrim's Progress*. Harmondsworth: Penguin, 1965.

Brehaut-Ryerson, Stanley. *Le capitalisme et la Confédération: aux sources du conflit Canada-Québec (1760-1873)*. Montréal: Éditions Parti Pris, 1972.

Cardwell, J. D., and K. A. Kalab. "Searching for the Theoretical Godot: A Plea for Theoretical Diversity in Modern Sociology." *Sociological Focus* 19, 2 (April 1986): 207-14.

Cassirer, Ernst. *Language and Myth*. Translated by S. Langer. New York: Dover, 1953.

Caws, Mary Ann. *The Eye in the Text: Essays on Perception, Mannerist to Modern*. Princeton: Princeton University Press, 1981.

Chua, Beng-Huat. "Democracy as a Textual Accomplishment." *The Sociological Quarterly* 20 (Autumn 1979): 541-49.

Clark, Joseph. *An Invitation to Help Build a Better Canada / Une invitation à batir ensemble l'avenir du Canada*. Ottawa: Constitutional Affairs Canada, 1992.

Clifford, Gay. *The Transformations of Allegory*. London and Boston: Routledge & Kegan Paul, 1974.

Comte, Auguste. *A General View of Positivism*. Translated by J. H. Bridges. New York: Speller, 1975.

Coutler, Jeff. "Beliefs and Practical Understanding." In *Everyday Language: Studies in Ethnomethodology*, edited by G. Psathas, pp. 163-86. New York: Irvington, 1979.

————. "Perceptual Accounts and Interpretive Asymmetries." *Sociology* 3, 3 (1975): 385-96.

Crowe, Keith. *A History of the Original Peoples of Northern Canada*. Toronto: Arctic Institute of North America, 1974.

Curtis, Bruce. *Building the Educational State: Canada West, 1836-1971*. London, ON: Falmer/Althouse, 1988.

————. "The Speller Expelled: Disciplining the Common Reader in Canada West." *The Canadian Review of Sociology and Anthropology* 22 (August 1985): 346-68.

de France, Marie. *French Medieval Romances*. Translated by Eugene Mason. London: Dent & Sons, 1932.

de Man, Paul. *Allegories of Reading: Figural Language in Rousseau, Nietzsche, Rilke and Proust*. New Haven and London: Yale University Press, 1979.

Department of Regional Industrial Expansion. *Think Canadian*. Hull: Ministry of Supplies and Services, 1985.

Department of the Secretary of State. *The Canadian Style: A Guide to Writing and Editing*. Toronto: Dundurn Press, 1985.

————. *The Report of the Task Force on Canadian Unity*, Vols. 1-3. Hull: Canadian Government Publishing, 1979.

————. *Canada Tomorrow Conference: Proceedings*. Hull: Canadian Government Publishing, 1983.

Derrida, Jacques. "Coming into One's Own." In *Psychoanalysis and the Question of the Text*, edited by G. Hartman, pp. 114-47. Baltimore: Johns Hopkins University Press, 1978.

————. "Languages and Institutions of Philosophy." *Semiotic Inquiry* 4, 2 (June 1984): 91-153.

————. "Living on Borderlines." In *Deconstruction and Criticism*, edited by H. Bloom, pp. 75-176. New York: Seabury Press, 1979.

————. *Margins of Philosophy*. Translated by Alan Bass. Chicago: University of Chicago Press, 1982.

————. *Of Grammatology*. Translated by G. C. Spivak. Baltimore: Johns Hopkins University Press, 1976.

————. *Otobiographies: l'enseignement de Nietzsche et la politique du nom propre*. Paris: Galiée, 1984.

————. *The Ear of the Other: Otobiography Transference Translation*. Edited by C.V. McDonald and translated by P. Kamuf and A. Ronell. New York: Schocken, 1985.

————. "The Law of Genre." *Glyph* 7 (1980): 202-32.

de Tocqueville, Alexis. *Democracy in America*. Edited by J. P. Mayer and translated by George Lawrence. Garden City, NY: Doubleday/Anchor, 1969.

Dictionary of Archaic and Provincial Words. London: John Russell Smith, 1878.

Dostoyevsky, Fyodor. *Notes From Underground & The Double*. Translated by Jessie Coulson. Harmondsworth: Penguin, 1972.

Douglas, Mary. *Purity and Danger: An Analysis of Concepts of Pollution and Taboo*. Harmondsworth: Penguin, 1970.

Eco, Umberto. "On Symbols." *Semiotic Inquiry* 2, 1 (March 1982): 15-44.

Eliade, Mircea. *Myths, Rites, Symbols: A Mircea Eliade Reader*. Edited by W. C. Beane and W. G. Doty. New York: Harper Colophon, 1975.

Everyman with Other Interludes including Eight Miracle Plays. London and Toronto: Dent/Dutton, 1930.

Fekete, John, ed. *The Structural Allegory: Reconstructive Encounters with the New French Thought*. Minneapolis: University of Minnesota Press, 1984.

Fish, Stanley. *Is There a Text in This Class? The Authority of Interpretive Communities*. Cambridge, MA: Harvard University Press, 1980.

Fletcher, Angus. *Allegory: The Theory of a Symbolic Mode*. Ithaca: Cornell University Press, 1980.

Foster, Hal. *The Anti-Aesthetic: Essays on Postmodern Culture*. Port Townsend, WA: Bay Press, 1983.

Foucault, Michel. *Language, Counter-Memory, Practice: Selected Essays and Interviews*. Edited by D. F. Bouchard and translated by D. F. Bouchard and S. Simon. Ithaca: Cornell University Press, 1977.

————. *The Order of Things: An Archaeology of the Human Sciences*. New York: Pantheon Books, 1971.

————. "What Is an Author?" In *Textual Strategies: Perspectives in Post-Structural Criticism*, translated and edited by J. Harari, pp. 141-60. Ithaca: Cornell University Press, 1979.

Freud, Sigmund. *Beyond the Pleasure Principle*. Edited and translated by J. Strachey. New York: W. W. Norton, 1961.

————. *Civilization and its Discontents*. Edited and translated by J. Strachey. New York: W. W. Norton, 1961.

————. *A General Introduction to Psychoanalysis*. Translated by J. Riviere. New York: Pocket Books, 1973.

————. *On Creativity and the Unconscious*. Edited and introduced by B. Nelson. New York: Harper & Row, 1958.

————. *The Interpretation of Dreams*. Edited and translated by J. Strachey. New York: Basic Books, 1955.

Friedrichs, Robert. *A Sociology of Sociology*. New York: Free Press, 1970.

Garfinkel, Harold. "The Origins of the Term 'Ethnomethodology.'" In *Ethnomethodology*, edited by Roy Turner, pp. 15-18. Harmondsworth: Penguin Books, 1974.

Garfinkel, Harold, et al. "The Work of a Discovering Science Construed with Materials from the Optically Discovered Pulsar." *Philosophy of the Social Sciences* 11 (1981): 131-58.

Gasché, Rudolph. "Deconstruction as Criticism." *Glyph* 6 (1979): 177-215.

_____. "Genres, Styles, and Figural Interpretation." *Glyph* 7 (1980): 102-30.

Gibbins, Roger. "Constitutional Politics in the West and the Rest." In *Confederation in Crisis*, edited by Robert Young, pp. 19-27. Toronto: Lorimer, 1991.

Godzich, W., and S. Spadaccini. *Literature Among Discourses: The Spanish Golden Age*. Minneapolis: University of Minnesota Press, 1986.

Goodman, Nelson. "The Status of Style." *Critical Inquiry* 1 (1975): 799-811.

Goodwin, Charles. "The Interactive Construction of a Sentence in Natural Conversation." In *Everyday Language: Studies in Ethnomethodology*, edited by G. Psathas, pp. 97-121. New York: Irvington, 1979.

Green, Bryan. *Knowing the Poor: A Case Study in Textual Reality Construction*. London: Routledge & Kegan Paul, 1983.

_____. "On the Evaluation of Social Theory." *Philosophy of the Social Sciences* 7 (1977): 33-50.

Harari, Josué, ed. *Textual Strategies: Perspectives in Post-Structural Criticism*. Ithaca, NY: Cornell University Press, 1979.

Hartman, Geoffrey. *Criticism in the Wilderness: The Study of Literature Today*. New Haven: Yale University Press, 1980.

_____. *The Unmediated Vision*. New York: Harcourt, Brace and World, 1966.

Heidegger, Martin. *What is Philosophy?* Translated and introduced by W. Kluback and J. T. Wilde. Great Britain: Twayne, 1958.

Hobbes, Thomas. *Leviathan*. Harmondsworth: Penguin Books, 1981.

Holland, Norman. *5 Readers Reading*. New Haven: Yale University Press, 1975.

_____. *Poems in Persons*. New York: W. W. Norton, 1973.

James, William. *The Principles of Psychology*, Vol. 1. New York: Dover, 1950.

Kalmar, Ivan. "A Note on the Inadequacy of Modern Socio-Political Terms in the Inuit Language." Paper presented to the Third Forum on Interdisciplinary Studies, Cancun, Mexico, 1983.

Kerr, W. P. *English Literature: Medieval*. London: Williams & Norgate, [n.d.].

Kristeva, Julia. *Desire in Language: A Semiotic Approach to Literature and Art*. Edited by L. Roudiez and translated by T. Gora, et al. New York: Columbia University Press, 1980.

Kroker, Arthur, and David Cook. *The Postmodern Scene: Excremental Culture and Hyper-Aesthetics*. Montreal: New World Perspectives, 1986.

Langer, Suzanne. *Philosophy in a New Key: A Study in the Symbolism of Reason, Rite and Art*. Cambridge, MA: Harvard University Press, 1978.

Langland, William. *Piers Plowman: The Vision of a People's Christ*. Edited by Arthur Burrell. New York: Dent/Dutton, 1912.

Leach, Edmund. *Culture and Communication: The Logic by Which Symbols Are Connected*. Cambridge: Cambridge University Press, 1976.

———. *Social Anthropology*. New York: Oxford, 1982.

———. "The Big Fish in the Biblical Wilderness." *The International Review of Psychoanalysis* 13 (1986): 129-40.

Le Goff, Jacques. *The Medieval Imagination*. Translated by Arthur Goldhammer. Chicago: University of Chicago Press, 1988.

Leitch, Vincent. *Deconstructive Criticism: An Advanced Introduction*. New York: Columbia University Press, 1976.

Levin, Samuel. "Allegorical Language." In *Allegory, Myth and Symbol*, edited by M. W. Bloomfield, pp. 23-38. Cambridge, MA: Harvard University Press, 1981.

Luckmann, Thomas, ed. *Phenomenology and Sociology*. London: Penguin, 1978.

Lyotard, Jean-François, *The Inhuman: Reflections on Time*. Translated by G. Bennington and R. Bowlby. Stanford: Stanford University Press, 1991.

Machiavelli, Niccolo. *The Prince and the Discourses*. New York: Modern Library, 1940.

Macpherson, C. B. *The Political Theory of Possessive Individualism: From Hobbes to Locke*. Oxford: Oxford University Press, 1964.

Malinowski, Bronislaw. *Magic, Science and Religion and Other Essays*. New York: Doubleday Anchor Books, 1954.

McHoul, Alex. *Telling How Texts Talk: Essays on Reading and Ethnomethodology*. London: Routledge & Kegan Paul, 1982.

McLuhan, Marshall. "Interview." *Maclean's* 9, 5 (1977): 4-9.

Melnyk, George. *Radical Regionalism*. Edmonton: NeWest Press, 1981.

Mitchell, D. *The Process of Reading: A Cognitive Analysis of Fluent Reading and Learning to Read*. Chichester: John Wiley & Sons, 1982.

Morgan, Edmund. *Inventing the People: The Rise of Popular Sovereignty in England and America*. New York: W. W. Norton, 1988.

Morrison, Kenneth. "Reader's Work: Devices for Achieving Pedagogic Events in Textual Materials for Readers as Novices to Sociology." Doctoral Dissertation, York University, 1976.

———. "Some Properties of 'Telling-Order Designs' in Didactic Inquiry." *Philosophy of the Social Sciences* 11 (1981): 245-62.

Morrow, Raymond. "Critical Theory and Critical Sociology." *Canadian Review of Sociology and Anthropology* 22, 5 (December 1985): 710-47.

Natanson, Maurice. *Phenomenology and Social Reality*. The Hague: Martinus Nijhoff, 1970.

Newman, Peter C. "The Good News from Robarts and Pepin: Canada, the Uncountry, Can Be Reinvented." *Maclean's* 92, 6 (1979): 3.

Nielsen, Greg. "Reading the Quebec Imaginary: Marcel Rioux and Dialogical Form." *Canadian Journal of Sociology* 12, 1-2 (1987): 134-49.

Nietzsche, Friedrich. *The Use and Abuse of History*. Translated by A. Collins. Indianapolis: Bobbs-Merrill, 1957.

————. *Thus Spoke Zarathustra*. Translated by R. J. Hollingsdale. Harmondsworth: Penguin, 1961.

Official Languages Act. *Revised Statutes of Canada* 5 (1970): 5581-99.

O'Neill, John. *Essaying Montaigne: A Study of the Institution of Reading and Writing*. London and Boston: Routledge & Kegan Paul, 1982.

————. *Five Bodies: The Human Shape of Modern Society*. Ithaca, NY: Cornell University Press, 1985.

Parsons, Talcott. *The Social System*. New York: Free Press of Glencoe, 1951.

Pollner, Melvin. "Mundane Reasoning." *Philosophy of the Social Sciences* 4 (1974): 35-54.

Pownall, Thomas. *The Administration of the British Colonies*. Albany: [n.p.], 1764.

Psathas, George, ed. *Everyday Language: Studies in Ethnomethodology*. New York: Irvington, 1979.

————. *Phenomenological Sociology: Issues and Apllications*. New York: John Wiley & Sons, 1973.

Redner, Harold. *The Ends of Philosophy: A Study in the Sociology of Philosophy and Rationality*. London: Croom Helm, 1986.

Report of the Royal Commission on Bilingualism and Biculturalism, The, Vols. 1-5. Ottawa: Queen's Printer, 1967-70.

Resnick, Philip. *Toward a Canada-Quebec Union*. Montreal and Kingston: McGill-Queen's University Press, 1991.

Ricoeur, Paul. *Interpretation Theory: Discourse and the Surplus of Meaning*. Fort Worth: Texas Christian University Press, 1976.

————. "The Model of the Text: Meaningful Action Considered as a Text." In *Interpretive Social Science*, edited by P. Rabinow and W. Sullivan, pp. 73-101. Berkeley: University of California Press, 1979.

Roche, Maurice. *Phenomenology, Language and the Social Sciences*. London and Boston: Routledge & Kegan Paul, 1973.

Rosmarin, Adena. *The Power of Genre*. Minneapolis: University of Minnesota Press, 1985.

Schouls, Peter. *The Imposition of Method: A Study of Descartes and Locke*. Oxford: Clarendon Press, 1980.

Schutz, Alfred. *Reflections on the Problem of Relevance.* Edited by R. Zaner. New Haven and London: Yale University Press, 1970.

Simmel, Georg. *The Sociology of Georg Simmel.* Edited by K. Wolff. New York: Free Press, 1950.

Silverman, D., and B. Torode. *The Material Word: Some Theories of Language and Its Limits.* London: Routledge & Kegan Paul, 1980.

Smith, Dorothy. "K is Mentally Ill: The Anatomy of a Factual Account." *Sociology* 12, 1 (1978): 10-25.

_____. "No One Commits Suicide: Textual Analysis of Ideological Practices." *Human Studies* 6 (1983): 309-59.

_____. "Textually-Mediated Social Organization." *International Social Science Journal* 36, 1 (1984): 59-74.

_____. "The Active Text: A Textual Analysis of the Social Relations of Public Textual Discourse." Paper presented to the World Congress of Sociology in Mexico City, August 1982.

_____. "The Ideological Practice of Sociology." *Catalyst* 2 (Winter 1974): 39-54.

_____. "The Intersubjective Structuring of Time." *Analytic Sociology* 1, 1 (1979): 10-25.

_____. "The Social Construction of Documentary Reality." *Sociological Inquiry* 44, 4 (1974): 257-68.

_____. "Women's Perspective as a Radical Critique of Sociology." *Sociological Inquiry* 44, 1 (1974): 7-13.

Spencer, Herbert. *On Social Evolution.* Edited and introduced by J. D. Y. Peel. Chicago: University of Chicago Press, 1972.

Sprigge, T. L. S. *Theories of Existence.* Harmondsworth: Penguin Books, 1984.

Thibault, Paul. *Text, Discourse and Context: A Social Semiotic Perspective.* Toronto: Victoria University Monograph, 1986.

Thompson, John B. *Critical Hermeneutics: A Study in the Thought of Paul Ricoeur and Jurgen Habermas.* Cambridge: Cambridge University Press, 1981.

Toller, T. N., ed. *An Anglo-Saxon Dictionary.* Oxford: Oxford University Press, 1954.

Tomasello, Andrew. *Music and Ritual in Papal Avignon, 1309-1403.* Ann Arbor: University of Michigan Research Press, 1983.

Trudeau, Pierre E. "Interview." *Maclean's* 90, 1 (1977): 4-8.

Turner, Bryan. *The Body & Society: Explorations in Social Theory.* Oxford: Basil Blackwell, 1984.

Turner, Roy. "Speech and the Social Contract." *Inquiry* (1985): 28-53.

_____. "Words, Utterances and Activities." In *Understanding Everyday Life*, edited by J. Douglas, pp. 165-87. Chicago: Aldine, 1970.

Turner, Roy, ed. *Ethnomethodology.* Harmondsworth: Penguin Books, 1974.

Tyler, Stephen. "Ethnography, Intertextuality and the End of Description." *American Journal of Semiotics* 3, 4 (1985): 93-98.

Ulmer, Gregory. *Applied Grammatology*. Baltimore: Johns Hopkins University Press, 1985.

Waite, P. B. *The Life and Times of Confederation 1864-1867*. Toronto and Buffalo: University of Toronto Press, 1962.

Webster's Third New International Dictionary. Springfield, MA: G. & C. Merriam, 1961.

Wilden, Anthony. *The Imaginary Canadian: An Examination for Discovery*. Vancouver: Pulp Press, 1980.

Wittgenstein, Ludwig. *On Certainty*. New York: Harper Torchbooks, 1972.

Index